SOCIAL CONTROL AT OPPORTUNITY BOYS' HOME

How Staff Control Juvenile Inmates

Paul-Jahi Christopher Price

University Press of America,® Inc.
Lanham · Boulder · New York · Toronto · Oxford

Copyright © 2005 by
University Press of America,® Inc.
4501 Forbes Boulevard
Suite 200
Lanham, Maryland 20706
UPA Acquisitions Department (301) 459-3366

PO Box 317
Oxford
OX2 9RU, UK

Library of Congress Control Number: 2004114181
ISBN 0-7618-3063-4 (paperback : alk. ppr.)

Contents

Preface

Juvenile delinquency has intrigued me since undergraduate school. I participated in an interim juvenile hall program at Riverside Juvenile Hall, which was very interesting. For one month, our class visited and observed various juvenile facilities, talking with probation officers, counselors, guards, social workers, juvenile inmates, teachers employed by Riverside Juvenile Hall and recreation staff. The facilities varied from placement centers to group homes to juvenile halls. We received a good sense of detention or facility types for teenagers.

As a group of seven students and one faculty, we met weekly discussing our observations and journal entries. Frequently, our discussions focused on juvenile offenses, causes and consequences of criminality. We had little knowledge of policy or treatment, but we knew their experience was different from our own. That is, we were university students exploring someone else's social world, exploring someone else's environment. We were fascinated by their eagerness, and willingness to share with us. Our encounters with juveniles were reciprocal, that is, we desired to know much about each other.

While their experience appeared "normal," it was not permanent. Most juveniles aspired to leave placement returning home to a more mainstream lifestyle. They discussed educational, occupational and social goals; many supported and expressed a Mertonian attitude of material success and taking advantage of opportunities.

My undertaking of this project (OBH research) is the fulfillment of a long held interest and fascination. That is, I wanted to uncover "what is *really* going on in there!" My interest then is to obtain an understanding of staff and juveniles from a very human, firsthand and personal standpoint. What are their concerns? What do they worry about? How are they connected to the institution? What relationships are established among members of the institution? And how does the institution affect their perception of self, life and detention?

One intention through this work is to provide a guide to (and understanding of) social control. There is no better place to observe, learn, strategize and practice social control than in correctional institutions. Opportunity Boys' Home (OBH) provides a wealth of information and experiences on the process of social control. That is, how is social control constructed and managed? Such information must be exposed and presented to the larger community. Social control in and of itself means nothing without understanding the structure from which it emanates. That is, a guide to social control is designed to teach order, maintenance of order, appropriate interaction with authority, and respect for organization. Keeping in mind that every setting develops ways of handling control issues, yet the fundamental similarity is control, e.g., if order is disrupted, control is near.

Part of this analysis examines "junior staff," e.g., juvenile inmates (residents) who assist staff and those who have internalized institutional ideas and philosophies. "Junior Staff" take it upon themselves to practice and maintain order. In short, they have bought into a system that they "accept"; moreover the "junior staff" position is usually a means to an end, e.g., some type of reward. As a guide then, how do staff attract junior staff? For attracting and "hiring" junior staff make staff responsibility much easier.

Problematic among juvenile inmates (or residents) is their historical lack of discipline. Countless counseling sessions and interviews reveal that parents, teachers and guardians had very little control of youth. In some cases "authority figures" were frightened by juveniles, while other control officials were unavailable, having few resources to employ assistance. How can institutions of control treat this lack of discipline and develop a healthy respect for authority?

Is it possible to teach order and discipline to juvenile inmates (residents)? Of course! This investigation demonstrates that juveniles are searching for someone to establish order, someone who is firm and in charge. Staff firmness provides feelings of security for juveniles; they feel protected by staff. Youth desire guidance, acceptance and approval from control officials. Teaching order is not only possible but desired by juveniles. Residents are more likely to respond to authority when staff establish and maintain control. In the long run, residents (juveniles) favor environments that are predictable and therefore stable.

Ethnography is very influential in discovery and essential to my research strategy. This method permits a first hand, qualitative approach; an approach that makes sense given my concern with control; an approach that lends itself to interaction, participation and interpretation of events; an approach that examines detail of instances; an approach that placed this researcher at center stage. Ethnographically, center stage is a valuable research position, for it allows access to encounters and access to information, both of which are cited in manuscript. The value of this approach lies in its flexibility to researchers. That is, ethnographers may explore and compare encounters; question and critically think though incidents. Here, one may develop a unique research style that is relevant to the specific situation under study.

In addition to fulfilling a long held interest, this project is designed to assist other control institutions in managing control. Specifically, placement facilities and group homes are my primary focus; it is hoped that such institutions benefit from my observations, analyses and solutions. Social control is a central part of juvenile halls, prisons, jails, placement-centers and group homes; without sufficient control ability, control institutions would dissolve into chaos. Alternatively, superior control enhances order, security and the opportunity to achieve treatment and institutional goals.

The value of this study has implications for other institutions whose emphasis is not primarily control. That is, parents control children, teachers control students, employers control employees, coaches control players, doctors control patients, etc. While each setting is distinct, there is an overriding similarity of maintaining order and conformity to get things done. Thus, it is with these concerns that I approach this project.

Paul-Jahi Christopher Price

Chapter 1

Opportunity Boys' Home:
An Introduction

Paul C. Price

Community-based group homes for incarcerating and/or treating delinquent youth are growing in numbers and provide increasingly important alternatives for the care and treatment of delinquent and other youth. Increased importance of group homes is in turn an outcome of the implementation of the policies of deinstitutionalization (Lewis et al, 1991). Deinstitutionalization advocates assert that group homes and other new community based treatment programs will "avert the many abuses that were regularly occurring in large state-run institutions and that the smaller, localized treatment environments would produce better outcomes for clients" (Krisberg, 1988:9).

Despite the hopes and claims of success with deinstitutionalization, criticisms remain concerning the way this new system of care operates. For instance, there are important criticisms about the quality of care in private programs, the longer average stays in private facilities, and the apparent discriminatory tendency to place white youth in private programs and minority youngsters in public facilities (Krisberg, 1988). These problems raise troubling questions about providers of group home care, and more generally, deinstitutionalization.

This research contributes to an understanding of contemporary policies of deinstitutionalization by examining the daily operations of one central institution in this emergent system, the group home. Indeed, more knowledge is necessary about the functioning of group homes, given their increased importance in care and treatment of delinquent youth, and growth in their resident populations and in the numbers of people employed as staff.

I do not however, examine every aspect of group homes. My interest is not treatment successes or failures, nor is it resident (e.g., inmate) perceptions of group homes. Rather, I examine staff activities. Specifically, I look at staff who have most direct and frequent contact with "clients". The activities of such frontline staff (Lipsky, 1980) critically shape and determine the character and functioning of group homes.

Thus, this book examines routine work practices of the frontline staff of a residential treatment program for delinquent youth. In this respect, the sociology of work is an integral part of this study. That is, I critically analyze what staff *do*, and what their work involves. While there are many components to the work of frontline staff in such institutions, its core activities involve the direct management and control of delinquent youth. That is, frontline staff are formal social control agents who are primarily involved in "control-work," e.g., breaking up fights, resolving resident conflicts, negotiating order, maintaining straight lines, confronting rule violations by residents, and responding to emergencies. In short, "control-work" involves maintaining order, which represents an end in itself for frontline staff in residential treatment settings.[1]

The importance of control-work in group-homes is illustrated by a recent report in the *Los Angeles Times* on the closing of a group home for delinquent youth. Pride House group home was closed because authorities felt that the home and its staff were not effectively controlling residents. Los Angeles County officials indicated that "the problem was the level of supervision." That is, "we want these acting-out teenagers supervised and not just wandering around" (Rainey & Cardenas, 1996). The article cites two cases of poor control:

> In one, several youths were chased back to the campus by LAPD for being absent without leave. There, some of the residents angrily confronted the officers and made obscene gestures, leading to the arrest of one. In the second incident, a young woman sneaking out of the facility fell from the second-story window and fractured her vertebrae.[2]

While poor control-work may shutdown certain group homes, control-work that is too strict and authoritarian can lead to resident complaints. Specifically, the Pride House inquiry further revealed that seven of ten residents complained that "staff seemed preoccupied with discipline and did not give them positive attention" (Rainey & Cardenas, 1996). Staff then are confronted with an annoying dilemma, e.g., how does one define and maintain appropriate (mid-range) control measures? Clearly, staff must control, but they can not do so in overly punitive ways. In group-homes, moreover, such control must reflect treatment, in that infractions should be corrected by using behavior-altering sanctions.

My analysis examines control-work practices of the frontline staff of one particular group home for delinquent youth, Opportunity Boys' Home (OBH). Opportunity Boys' Home is a small private community-based facility that proposes to treat delinquent tendencies in youth. But studying these practices in one setting nonetheless has broader sociological implications. For instance, we learn about the work processes of a neglected yet interesting occupational group, i.e., frontline staff in a group home. We experience their work by going inside their work environment (inside staff/resident encounters), examining how certain control decisions emerge and how they are enforced.

Further, we learn about how a key juvenile institution, the placement facility, actually functions, especially from the standpoint of its frontline staff. How do they understand their work and the institutional context within which it occurs? More importantly, how do they go about managing and controlling residents of OBH under the constraints and supervision of Home administrators? What are their strategies and tactics for maintaining order, and how do they decide when to use one rather than the another? These are central questions that are addressed in the book, given the perceptions and experiences of staff are significant focal points when analyzing institutional social control processes.

In looking at the control-work of frontline staff, we can also understand the creation of a "negotiated order" (Strauss et. al, 1963) in the group home. Here, staff may overlook certain norm violations by residents as a trade-off for good behavior. But this is a negotiated process. How does it occur? Examining residential infractions that can be ignored, acknowledged and confronted by staff, depending upon the situation and those involved, furthers our understanding of the bargaining process.

Finally, we learn more about social control and how it is actually carried out on a day to day and moment by moment basis in an institution devoted to such control. In this respect, Opportunity Boys' Home is both an institution of social control, and an institution that has its own internal social control mechanisms (punishments, rewards, etc) that have many similarities with the control mechanisms in other institutions like families or schools that do not specialize in social control.

On Juvenile Institutions

Little research has been carried out on the social control process in juvenile institutions. While researchers (Studt, et al, 1968; Irwin, 1980; Kauffman, 1988; Useem & Kimball, 1989) have extensively examined the staff world in adult prisons, through surveys and interviews, few researchers (Polsky, 1962; Feld, 1977; Buckholdt & Gubrium, 1979) have addressed the staff world in a juvenile detention placement facility. Clearly, there are many similarities between adult and juvenile institutions: low wages, physical and emotional strain, burn-out, long hours, head counts and contraband searches. But there are important differences that make staff working in a juvenile placement facility distinctive. For example, the treatment orientation and the community-based character of these programs for youth are quite different from what is practiced in most prisons. There has never been an organized collective protest by OBH residents; and, the kinds of social relations between staff and resident are more intimate than in adult prisons. Finally, community-based programs, like Opportunity Boys' Home, are not locked-down, so staff are confronted with awols (or escapes) and the threat of awols more frequently.

Some studies have looked at treatment and comparable institutions in terms of the distinctive work situations confronted by staff. Landers (1986), in his discussion of "Juvenile Justice Inside or Out," recognized that staff working in juvenile halls and community-based group homes are involved in "people work" (Goffman, 1961), e.g., the object & product of staff work are people. In doing people work, staff exercise authority by threat, reward, persuasion, coercion and manipulation (Kauffman, 1988). However, by "working on people" (Hasenfeld, 1983), staff may develop emotional feelings for clients, realizing that human persons experience pain, joy, love, and compassion, which are all tied to the institution. For this reason, the quality of people work determines the overall reaction of staff to inmates and vice versa.

For McDermott & King (1988), part of staff work consists of "mind games" or "head games." That is staff and inmates are frequently involved in a variation of mind games in order to establish control, to survive, to register grievances, to acquire unearned privileges and to avoid work. Mind games are an important part of staff work, for it is here that staff are required to match wits with inmates; in so doing, staff display their knowledge and understanding of correctional systems, gaining respect or contempt from inmates. Mind games further suggest that every action is not physical, e.g., staff must learn how to diffuse potentially violent situations (Infantino & Musingo, 1985).

Clearly, research on juvenile placement facilities is limited. No juvenile residential institution has ever been holistically studied, for it is a huge task to analyze every issue that surfaces during the course of study. But the deficiency in literature pertaining to staff in juvenile placements facilities, and even in juvenile halls, is striking; these are areas of investigation that require close study. Here then, uncovering information on community-based juvenile facilities is crucial, for as much as possible, such study will broaden our knowledge, help direct future research, using creative methodologies, and hopefully inspire new placement policies and procedures.

On Deinstitutionalization

Intensive study of group homes for delinquent youth is quite significant, because these types of placement facilities are key institutions in the new system of deinstitutionalized care for delinquents. Study of deinstitutionalization programs gets at the importance of re-labeling status offenders to maintain control over them (Empey & Stafford, 1991:478) and provide more optimistic perceptions of status offenders. Community-based programs often refer to their clients as residents, not inmates, while internal housing facilities are called dorms or cottages rather than units. Even staff members are relabeled as counselors and social workers not guards.

Furthermore, social control at community-based institutions is different from that characteristic of prisons in that staff may not use physical force, the facility structure is relatively open, as opposed to lock-down, and residents may awol at any time. These conditions compel staff to be particularly innovative when doing control.

While community-based group homes for delinquent youth have some of the characteristics of Goffman's description of total institutions (1964:4), they lack others. Such institutions refer to settings that are not entirely closed and separated from the outside world; indeed, many are community-based. Physical restraints and boundaries are not necessarily present; boundaries and restraints are more psychological. But there are some very key similarities, including rigid rules, involuntary admittance, informal rules, standardized food and activities, residents managed and regulated by staff. Such facilities, including court ordered placement facilities, group homes and halfway houses, might better be termed "semi-total institutions".

On Negotiation

Additionally, this investigation examines how order is produced and maintained in one institution by focusing on frontline staff's definitions of and responses to deviant behavior by its residents. Order however does not simply exist, it must be "worked at" (Strauss et. al, 1963). Order is "reconstituted continually" (Strauss et. al, 1963) during every encounter; and negotiation (give and take) plays an important role in how order is established and maintained in these encounters. The type of order that exists in any institution is in part shaped by these negotiations and their outcomes.

Bazerman and Neale (1992) recognize that "everyone negotiates." It occurs between all sorts of people and in varying contexts, e.g., in boardrooms, prisons, detention centers, probation offices, hallways, courts, airplanes, cars, tennis courts, on telephones, in the media, etc. The items and/or issues of negotiation also vary. For instance, cars, salaries, hostages, peace, childhood bedtime, teenage curfew, grammatical terms, phrases, movies, inmate order, and player trades. In short, most "things" are negotiable. "Negotiation [then] is a process, the objective of which is to find a mutually acceptable compromise"(Bartos, 1974:298). In the case of OBH, part of control is to negotiate order.

According to Spencer (1987), probation officers are involved in face-to-face negotiations with defendants when deciding what sentence to recommend. "They engaged defendants in a process of negotiation aimed at reaching a shared agreement, which at least approximated the Pos' notions of propriety or acceptability" (Spencer, 1987:170). Probation officers recognize that defendants have distinctive interpretations and attitudes concerning their offenses and consequences. These perceptions and attitudes are taken into account when deciding on what sentence to recommend. Consequently, the process of negotiation, sometimes, involves "face-saving" and "face-restoration" (Goffman, 1959; Brown, 1977). Dispute deadlocks may have little to do with substantive issues, and more do with saving face from embarrassment, misunderstandings and mistakes in negotiation. Face-maintenance is significant in that no-one wants to be viewed as weak or foolish. Negotiations that continue without saving-face may yield advantages to negotiators who appear experienced, and cast doubt on inexperienced negotiators. Thus, negotiation of issues, and outcomes may stall until face-restoration is established (Brown, 1977).

Approaches to Social Control

All social institutions are concerned with social control. It helps to facilitate order and organization. It provides a structure to social interaction; rules and norms emerge from control encounters. Hence, the concern with social control is very real, while families, businesses, schools, churches, mental hospitals, juvenile halls and group homes all rely on formal and informal control processes.

Wisely, Edward Ross (1901) identified and utilized social control as a sociological concept. Then, social control referred to all human practices and arrangements that contribute to social order and influence people to conform. Law, custom and religion have typically contributed to social order and influencing individuals to conform. On the one hand social control is formalized through laws and judicial systems; on the other hand, social control might be informal through custom, peer pressure and internalization of norms. Here, social control penetrates the very essence of society; it has an effect on everything we do.

Parsons (1964) argued that there is a close relationship between social control and socialization; theorists then should consider taking "certain features of the processes of socialization as a point of reference for developing a framework for the analysis of social control" (Parson, 1964:298). He further maintained that preventive aspects of social control consist of processes which teach actors not to embark on processes of deviance (Parsons, 1964). Hence, the most basic part of the social control apparatus is an invisible part of everyday life. That is, "if society is functioning effectively, most of its members will be guided by internalize standards of conduct that they share with others and that fall within the normative boundaries of the system, and will feel uncomfortable at even the thought of violating those standards" (Wheeler, 1973:685).

On another level, Parsons (1967) examines social control through the use of force. "Force is a way of trying to 'make sure' that alters act in a desired manner, or refrains from acting in an undesired one" (Parsons, 1967:268). Lemert (1967) agrees that force is sometimes used as a mode of social control, citing a type of "active social control." That is, active social control is formal in that conventional criminal justice agencies (police, judges, etc) are created to enforce compliance. Ultimately then, the use of force, as a social control method, is a means of direct or indirect deterrence.

Clearly, Ross, Parsons, Wheeler and others are discussing preventive social control; that is, control designed to prevent wrongdoings before they occur, whether through force or socialization. Labeling theorists tend to focus on reactive rather than preventive social control. Gibbs, for example, provides a reactive definition of deviance by arguing "a particular act is deviant, if and only if, it is reacted to distinctively (e.g., punitively) or 'so labeled' by at least one member of the social unit in question" (1981:25)[emphasis added]. Additionally, Black (1984) developed an explicit interactionist-reactive approach to social control, defining such control more narrowly as specific reactions to deviant behavior. In his view, social control involves the definition and response to deviant acts. "Social control itself proves to be only a limited instance of a larger phenomenon: evaluation" (Black, 1984:27). We must recognize that people apply standards to everything; "whether the standard refers to what is good or bad, true or false, or what is useful, delightful, or disgusting, all of this and more is *evaluation*" (Black, 1984). Social control then, is attached to evaluation by its normative character, e.g., its standards of right and wrong. There is a tendency for social control agents to react to deviance, e.g., their perception of "wrongness." Black (1984) identifies three major modes of evaluation in which people make value judgments, e.g., normative, intellectual and aesthetic. [3] Situationally then, one could receive all evaluation modes in a single environment, event or incident.

Definitions of deviant behavior are constructed by members within specific settings, responses, in turn, may reflect one's definition of what is deviant. Defining social control thus involves human interpretation and perception of what is deviant and consequently rests on subjective values. Clearly, definitions of what is deviant will vary widely from situation to situation, and institution to institution, but the reactive process is key to understanding Black's notion of social control, e.g., reactivity in the sense that social control agents respond to their view of inappropriate behavior by doing something about it.

It is reasonable then to argue that social control is a process involving definition, then response. Within the context of social control encounters, a formalized response may emerge. Moreover, within this same context an informal response might unfold. Thus, to what extent is a person's response to deviance rigid? Or, in what ways is a person's response to deviance situational? In short, after defining a situation as deviant, how do authority figures respond? What types of responses are available to authority figures? Generally, how one defines and responds to deviance depends on the institution, the situation, those involved and those watching. These are important considerations for an examination of social control, and social control agents who manage deviance.

Book Overview

The use of reactive social control theory is significant because it draws attention to the situational nature of staff work. Further, social control work at community-based group homes for delinquent youth is unlike staff social control work at state-run institutions. In short, the philosophies and reactions by staff are different, e.g., community-based programs emphasize deinstitutionalization while state-run institutions stress confinement. A theory of reactive social control gets at the nature of staff work in community-based programs, where "looser," more open structure allows staff more discretion to react in different ways.

This monograph examines several issues related to the "control-work" of OBH staff, e.g., learning control, everyday control, institutional emergencies and leaving control institutions. The aforementioned are the major chapters under examination. Social control makes up one major feature of staff work at Opportunity Boys' Home. This work consists of counseling residents, monitoring dorms, enforcing institutional rules, breaking up fights, issuing sanctions, bedding down residents, conducting group, etc. "Learning control" examines how control is learned by staff, e.g., through observing other staff, making mistakes and other strategies of learning.

"Everyday control" explores how order is maintained by doing control in everyday circumstances. Everyday or routine control gets at the process of maintaining order and conformity within the OBH institutional structure. Order is created and maintained daily; formal rules help to structure behavior and staff/resident interactions, but rules and order are often negotiated. Staff are charged with enforcing rules and with control more broadly; how exactly is this done?

An analysis of the panic button gets at how staff actually respond to institutional emergencies, e.g., an examination of how staff restore order during crisis situations. Here, it is interesting to explore how roles emerge during emergencies. One's formal status may have little to do with their acquired role during emergencies. Additionally, this chapter examines the process by which staff rush to the scene, respond to false alarms (or false emergencies) and resolve crises.

Finally, I examine the process of resident awols, and resident terminations to juvenile hall. Awols and terminations focus on "leaving" the facility, either voluntarily or involuntarily. Awols indicate that residents leave without permission, while residents who are terminated are forced to leave. Both may return, and many do, but "resident leaving" appears to temporarily relieve staff of inappropriate, and sometimes nerve-racking behavior by residents. Those residents who graduate[4] are perceived as successfully leaving, yet a negative stigma is attached to those who awol or terminate. Here, I explore the sociological significance of leaving (e.g., awoling & termination) an enclosed semi-total institution.

Notes

1. Unlike these frontline staff, most elementary school teachers are principally involved in teaching, not control. "Control-work" for teachers becomes a means to an end; that is, teachers cannot teach without classroom control (Denscombe, 1985).

2. See Rainey and Cardenas' (1996) article on "Youth Removed From Van Nuys Group Home."

3. Intellectually, individuals may be regarded as intelligent, insightful, inventive, smart, or as stupid or foolish. Aesthetic evaluation pertains to

what is worthy of appreciation, what is graceful, awesome, or distasteful, vulgar, or gross (Black, 1984).

4. Successfully complete the OBH program.

Chapter 2

Setting

Opportunity Boys' Home (OBH) is a placement facility that attempts to treat delinquent behavior of juvenile offenders. Treatment ranges from individual counseling, family counseling, group counseling, alcoholic and narcotic anonymous programs to psychiatric evaluations.[1] Treatment methods are in accordance with Home treatment philosophy and limited to the capabilities of staff. For example, Opportunity Boys' Home is a privately owned and operated institution which recruits the type of juvenile who best matches its treatment capabilities, and who are judged likely to successfully complete its program. Those admitted thus have usually committed such crimes as grand theft auto, petty theft, robbery, assault, school truancy, indecent exposure, possession and sale of narcotics. Conversely, this institution avoids most juveniles who have committed serious sexual or violent crimes, e.g., rape, child molestation and murder of any type.

More often than not, juveniles are recruited from the probation system and Juvenile Hall. Recruits range in age from thirteen to seventeen and their average OBH detention is approximately twelve months. When conversing with residents about their detention time (time frame), it is interesting how each juvenile can almost precisely recount his confinement months, although less precisely define their release or graduation date. There is a normal residential census of eighty-four, with African-Americans and Chicanos heavily represented, and to a lesser degree, Whites.

Using the term "resident" instead of inmate is consistent with the treatment principles of the Home. That is, inmate signifies a derogatory label implying confinement, menace to society and a need for punishment. The Home seeks to provide an environment and language that suggest individuals are normal, possessing abilities to function as productive members of society. The term "resident" is intended to make detainees feel better about themselves and modify their behavior. Resident further denotes a sense of community; the hope is to give residents a kind of emotional connection to Opportunity Boys' Home as their *home* and a sense of belonging to the surrounding community.

Opportunity is not a lock-down facility, as is Juvenile Hall. If residents decide to leave OBH without permission, their departure is usually without struggle, as staff are forbidden from restraining residents who wish to leave; yet, there are consequences to those who chose this option. Inside the institution, individual movement from dorm to dorm, or dorm to gym, does require a pass. In practice, however, residents often travel without valid passes and staff monitoring of passes is haphazard.[2]

A typical weekday schedule for residents begins with wake-up at 6:00am. Between wake-up and breakfast (6-6:30am), residents are required to sweep their rooms and make their beds, while staff supervise. After breakfast (7:00am), residents return to their dorms where they "thoroughly" clean it before school (8:00am). Staff, along with a high status resident, must inspect and approve rooms and dorm jobs. Rooms and dorm jobs that fail are re-done. Residents receive an hour lunch break in which they eat, most smoke, socialize and some watch TV. Schools ends at 2:00pm and group (group session) begins between 2:30pm & 3:00pm. Depending on the "issue(s)," a group-session could last for thirty minutes or several hours. Group is followed by free time until dinner at 5:30pm. Free time is also available after dinner (6:00pm), until study hour begins at 7:00pm. The final hour is again used at the discretion of residents; many chose to view television, write letters, play basketball, smoke cigarettes and/or shower before bed. Residents are in their rooms by 9:00pm and lights out at 9:15pm. Generally, this daily routine is followed by all residents, however; one important quality of semi-total institutions is that "caretakers" don't always adhere to institutional schedules.

The weekend schedule is more relaxed. For instance, residents are up at 7am. From 7am to 8am, residents shower and clean their rooms. Breakfast starts at 8am; after-which residents continue their room and dorm chores. On weekends, dorm and room inspection is not as thorough;

staff and high status residents typically "eye-ball" dorm jobs, passing them routinely. There is a short informative group session at 9:30. At 10am, residents who have earned home visits, begin checking out. Other residents are free to watch television, play in the gym or on the field, "laz" around the dorm, go to the recreation room or workshop. Lunch begins at 12 noon, and visiting hours for family and friends operates from 1pm to 4pm. Dinner starts at 5pm and another short group follows. After group, from 6pm to 11pm, residents engage in various activities; some "laz" around the dorm, others watch rented videos, at times, high status residents are chaperoned to the movies, or some other off site activity. Their day ends at 11pm, bedtime.

Facility Structure

Keeping with treatment concerns, residential housing is referred to as dorms rather than units or cells. There are five dorms at Opportunity Boys' Home--V, W, X, Y, & Z dorms. Though these letters have no specific meaning, staff and residents often informally re-label dorms by using the characterizations and personalities of staff and residents. For example, X-dorm is sometimes referred to as "animal house" because of its size (approximately 20 residents) and frequent chaos; while W-dorm is often referred to as "the baby dorm" because it houses the youngest residents.

Dorms house different quantities of residents. For instance, Z and X dorms hold twenty residents, V-dorm houses seventeen, Y-dorm accommodates sixteen and W-dorm carries twelve. In most cases, residents lodge two to a room while restrooms are typically communal. Z-dorm, which is the newest dorm, is the only dorm that has restrooms connected to rooms, e.g., rooms one and two, three and four, etc share the same restroom. Each dorm similarly contains a T.V. room (sometimes referred to as day room), staff office, broom closet and storage space. The day room receives the most usage in that many activities are conducted in this loca-tion. The day room is used for group sessions, dances, study sessions, television viewing, room substitution, family conferences and entertain-ment.

Dorms X, Y and Z are structurally connected, while V and W-dorms are linked. Note that X-Y-Z dorms are on the North side of the facility and V & W-dorms on the South side. The kitchen, various offices (O.D. office, nurse's office, secretary's office, executive director's office, a staff restroom), and lobby separates the V & W structures from X, Y & Z dorms. The institution is built in such a way that one can travel from V to Z-dorm without going outside the structure. And by opening the doors that separate X from Y-dorm and Y from Z-dorm, one can see from one end of the north side to the other. This is not the case with V & W dorms because V-dorm is built on top of W-dorm, thus one must use stairs to move from V to W-dorm.

In addition to dorms and offices, there are other buildings located on the complex: a school, gym, chapel, a house that lodges the executive director and four staff apartments which are built above the North dorms. The school is remedial, catering to the remedial academic levels of most OBH residents. Those residents who are above average and well behaved attend an off-campus school. Fran High School and OBH have an arrangement that permits high achieving OBH residents to attend FHS. Residents catch the bus to Fran High School, which is nearly three miles from OBH.

The gym contains a basketball court, a recently carpeted weight room, restrooms, showers that don't work, lockers that are not used, storage space, a canteen and an office. The gym houses the recreation department and its primary function is to provide ongoing activities for residents. This department has sponsored basketball, football, ping-pong, weight lifting tournaments; athletic teams are formed and compete against other placements. Movie outings, co-ed dances, game shows, camping trips, Dodger baseball games and fishing trips have been sponsored by recreation staff and enjoyed by residents.

Recreation department is further complimented with a fifteen-meter swimming pool, a craft workshop and a large playing field where football and baseball are played. Carnivals and rummage sales (fundraisers) are held annually on the playing field. Social workers and administrators place heavy emphasis on weekend activity, e.g., keeping residents busy.

A separate but related program at Opportunity Boys' Home is the Transitional Day Treatment Program (often referred to as TTP). Structurally, this program is above the gym and only operates during weekdays. It involves twenty residents (these residents are not included in the total population allotment) and six staff members, e.g., two staff are van drivers, a supervisor, a director and two family therapists. TTP participants do not live on campus but at home; they are transported daily to OBH. Some juveniles arrive by bus (RTD) while others are transported by OBH vehicles (vans). Participants are actually on campus from 8am to 5pm, attending school from 8am to 2pm, then conducting group from 2:30pm to 4:30pm and leaving by 5pm. Finally, TTP is very selective regarding its intake of juveniles, and like larger facilities, they obtain their residents from the juvenile hall system, from OBH itself and group homes owned by Opportunity Boys' Home.

Kitchen Structure and Meals

All meals are eaten in the dining area of the kitchen. Residents are required to eat with their dorms in an assigned section. Within the confines of their areas, residents are free to dine with selected peers. However, a consistent pattern of certain residents sitting together, and sitting in the same "place" has emerged. Interestingly enough, residents seem to assign themselves a dining room "space," separating themselves by race, gang affiliations and friendships. As part of staff work, they are required to dine among residents, monitoring their behavior.

There are three meals daily, beginning at 6:30am, 12:00n and 5:30pm. The Officer of the Day (O.D.) rings a bell five minutes before meals, as to alert dorms of meal time and a signal to prepare for dining. Before entering the kitchen, each dorm forms a straight line directly outside dining hall. The O.D. then inspects the straightness of dorm lines, resident attire and dorm mannerisms. Staff must accompany dorms to dining hall and assist by monitoring dorms. The O.D. selects the neatest and quietest dorm to enter the dining hall first. This dining entrance evaluation is done for each dorm until the final dorm has entered. Dorms that fail the entrance inspection are ordered back to their dorms to repeat kitchen line up. The inspection process has created a type of competition among dorms to enter first and receive institutional recognition as a well-mannered dorm.

After entering, each person files through a food line, selecting food from a prepared menu. While food is displayed in buffet style, the kitchen staff and crew are responsible for issuing appropriate portions—as residents and staff make their food choices. Moving further down the food line, individuals may pick-up salads, desserts and other food accessories. Each dorm, upon completing meals, leaves as a group; though depending on the dorm and their specific situation, staff may require that residents reform their line, walking collectively back to their dorm. Other staff permit their residents to loosely and individually return to their dwelling.

The kitchen crew is a component of the kitchen that sets up and cleans up after every meal. The kitchen crew is made up of residents whose job it is to wash dishes, mop and scrub floors, set foods out, buss tables and at times, serve food. For residents, working in the kitchen can be a constant source of income, albeit minimal. There is a pay differential among the positions of the working crew, e.g., the resident supervisor earns $2.00 per meal, his assistant $1.75 and regular workers earn $1.50 per meal. The role of the resident supervisor is to supervise, schedule and find replacements for his crew. The OBH kitchen staff is responsible for cooking, serving, supervising and monitoring the entire kitchen crew.

Social Services and Business Office

Separate from the dorms and kitchen lies a two-story building referred to as "social services" (A new "social services" building has been recently erected). This unit houses various administrative staff (Clinical director & Intake Worker), secretaries, switchboard operator, and counseling therapists. General staff meetings occur in the social service conference room, along with counseling sessions, in-service training, seminars and occasional staff parties.

Adjacent to social services and below Z-dorm rests the business office of Opportunity Boys' Home. Business employees have least interaction with residents, still they are responsible for resident accounts, dorm accounts, payroll and many other business concerns. The business office is awkwardly situated below Z-dorm. Consequently, business employees frequently complain of loud music and arguments emanating from this dorm.

OBH STAFF

Primarily, OBH staff includes administrators (executive director, clinical director, intake worker), O.D.s, and dorm staff (social workers, dorm coordinators, case aides, counselors, night staff). These groups have most contact with residents and are most directly responsible for social control and treatment. It is therefore useful to examine each group to describe their positions within the overall stratification structure of Opportunity Boys' Home.

Executive Director, Clinical Director and Intake Worker[3]

Executive director, Henry Nash, is well connected to Optimist Boys' Home. He is in charge of the entire OBH operation, relying on subordinate administrators, Officers of the Day (O.D.s), social workers and line staff to assist him.

Part of Nash's responsibility is to inform and interact with various Opportunity Clubs. Opportunity Clubs are made-up of volunteers (regular working citizens, seniors, politicians) who support the ideas and operation of OBH. There are fifteen such clubs throughout southern California, requiring an annual fee for membership. Club meetings are held every month in the OBH kitchen. These meetings give OBH members an opportunity to visit and tour the Home before meetings. When OBH club members arrive, Nash presents his "public relations" face. He sounds like a politician by speaking about rehabilitative efforts of staff and the effects of their efforts on residents. Usually a high status resident is requested to conduct tours of OBH, while dorms are notified in advance that an entourage is coming. Good tour guides are frequently tipped by Club visitors.

Nash is quite invested in the Home. He has lived and raised his family on the site since 1968. His residence is located on a hill above the Home, overlooking the entire Home from the rear. It is not unusual to see him walking the grounds or briefly in his office during weeknights and weekends. Directly below Henry's home are four staff apartments. Here, staff who are interested in filling vacancies must apply through Henry Nash; and usually, there are several applicants for one vacancy. Needless to say Henry plays a key role in determining who will reside in the rent-free apartments.

Henry interacts with every Home entity, e.g., residents, staff, O.D.s, administrators and club members. His status makes him the most powerful social control agent at OBH. He sanctions residents, staff, O.D.s, and administrators for positive contributions or negative drawbacks. He is aware of all major incidents and many minor troubles. His source of information comes from O.D.s, the main log, staff, administrators, residents, written reports (incident & awol reports) and his own visual observations. He's involved in staff disputes, certain staff terminations and resident dismissals. In short, Henry's "hands are in everything" at OBH.

The clinical director is primarily responsible for social workers, treatment philosophy of the Home, annual reports to the state and licensing contacts. Janette (clinical director) oversees and is directly responsible for social workers, e.g., she hires, orients, trains, evaluates, conducts meetings and terminates social workers. Additionally, the clinical director takes charge of identifying treatment philosophies and overseeing its implementation. Annual reports that are submitted to the state are usually compiled and written by Janette. When state licensing department inspects OBH (whether scheduled or unscheduled inspections), their first formal contact is with the Clinical director.

Further, Janette manages campus operations. That is, she has contact with line staff and residents. She occasionally attends, observes and conducts group sessions. When line staff and social workers are experiencing problems, Janette's intervention is often required. Transferring staff from one dorm to another to make dorms clinically stronger is often an unpopular decision made by Janette. The O.D.s primary contact with Janette concerns information. The O.D. typically xerox's incident reports for the executive, clinical and intake directors; she often wants an update of campus activities during evening and weekends (at times, she calls from her home wanting an update of a dorm or certain residents within dorms, and to convey messages to certain social workers). When investigating serious incidents (fights between residents and staff, parent consuming a resident's prescribed medication), Janette usually interviews all parties involved (staff, resident, parent, etc).

The intake worker, Inga, seems literally "all over the place," but probably more as a result to her personality than her institutional position. She is often on the scene during emergencies; she criticizes and attempts to influence new social workers; at times, she monitors meals, gym and school; she follows up on residential grievances, she observes, criticizes, and evaluates line staff; conducts group sessions with residents and staff; occasionally she is asked to resolve conflicts among residents and staff, or resident and resident; she clears the way for resident terminations and resident returns from juvenile hall. Social workers have complained about her meddling e.g., doing every body else's job and poorly doing her own. After hearing these complaints, Janette instructs her to limit her activity to her assigned responsibilities. Yet when the dust settles, Inga gradually returns to her meddlesome personality.

The intake worker is actually responsible for the recreation department, night staff, new staff orientation, O.D.s, and admission of new residents. She consults O.D.s to obtain an accurate count of residents; her concern is maintaining a full residential population, as is Henry's. In addition to reading the log, incident and awol reports, she consults O.D.s to obtain an overall feel of the Home. Those under her supervision are not impressed by her insensitive management approach. That is, in true working class fashion, Inga frequently scolds and talks down to her staff, and other employees. Contempt has developed from her management style; it is a style that threatens staff to "do it, or else!!" Interestingly, Inga displays an 8 x 11 flyer tapped to her desk lamp, which reads in bold letters: "Evolution of Authority." The sign depicts four separate footprints, beginning with an ape's foot print, then a human foot print, a man's contemporary shoe print and finally a female shoe print. Though some of their (administrators) roles overlap, Inga is third in command, taking orders from Henry and Janette.

Officer of the Day

The Officer of the Day (O.D.) performs a significant role in managing the Home. The administrative staff leaves by 6pm and thereafter, the O.D. assumes the administrative chore of being "in charge." Situations, like resident hospital visits or sending someone to juvenile hall, requiring O.D. assistance were either communicated to, discussed with, approved or disapproved by the Officer of the Day. In short, the O.D. functions as decision maker and task distributor.

The O.D. is required to walk through and inspect dorms, kitchen area, the gym and other areas of staff and resident activity. Executive director Henry Nash once commented: "O.D.'s should do more than sit behind a desk," and thus expects O.D.s to walk and oversee the institutional grounds. The O.D. carries a set of institutional keys that locks and unlocks most offices, dorms and departments on campus. The O.D. is formally required to distribute resident medications, answer phones, monitor the kitchen during meals, inspect & document the condition of Home vehicles, inform administrators of emergencies (riots, campus fires, vandalism) and assist dorm counselors when requested. Normally, dorm counselors request O.D. assistance when encountering fights between residents, threatening residents and chaotic dorms.

Located near the center of campus, the O.D. office contains a time clock and "main log." Most staff must daily pass through this office to sign in and out of the main log. This is done so that administrators might keep track of who and when staff arrive and depart. Yet, while official policy requires all staff to sign in and out, administrators *rarely* signed the log. In the privacy of their offices, administrators reviewed the log to receive a general sense of campus atmosphere (e.g., staff write-ups, dorm crises, vehicle status, etc). One is likely to read, in the log, accounts of non-functioning vehicles, residents transported to juvenile hall or hospital, recreational outings, resident graduations, resident awols, white glove clean up and on site visitors (resident relatives, probation officers, licensing).

By virtue of the office location and structure (the main log rests on the O.D. desk), the O.D. interacts at least minimally with most staff daily. The executive director has indicated that O.D.s should observe staff to determine their mental and physical condition. His primary concern is whether staff come to work intoxicated or smelling like alcohol. The previous O.D. frequently consumed alcohol during evening shifts. On occasion, some staff attend work intoxicated or shortly after drinking; and certain staff have been terminated due to intoxication or to admitted drinking before work. Henry seems to trust no one, thus if he suspects staff, he will periodically make surprise evening visits, conversing with staff at close proximity to determine their mental & physical conditions. The O.D., then, has power to deny an employee work, if he judges him a detriment to himself and others. In Henry's mind, apparently, the O.D. should be an extension of himself, that is, anything of significance should be reported to Henry (or some other administrator). And judging his suspicious gaze and silence, Henry seems to want O.D.'s to "snitch" on fellow staff.[4]

Dorm Staff and Their Role

Each dorm has a hierarchy of staff consisting of social workers, dorm coordinators, case aides and counselors. The dorm's population determines the number of staff assigned; a dorm of twenty residents contains a staff of six and a population of twelve, sixteen, or seventeen holds a working staff of five. Social workers along with administrators are responsible for hiring dorm staff, while the requirements for a dorm coordinator, case aide, or counselor stipulate a B.A. in psychology, sociology, social work (or some related field) and a year experience. Like other institutions, however, hiring guidelines and promotional considerations are sometimes compromised in the interest of "need." That is, certain dorm coordinators, case aides and counselors do not meet posted requirements, yet because of "extensive" experience and/or a claim to be in pursuit of a degree, positions may be granted.

Often, new staff enter Opportunity with a history of correctional employment. Some have worked at group homes, placement facilities, juvenile halls, and prisons. Others, who have no experience, enter OBH fresh out of college or some are simply seeking employment. Most staff entering OBH with experience eventually develop a desire to leave OBH, seeking employment in a related field, e.g., as a probation officer, juvenile hall counselor, correctional officer, or youth authority (Y.A.) counselor. All such areas promise better pay.

The racial make up of dorm staff reflects the residential population. Opportunity's diversified staff includes African Americans, Whites, and Chicanos. Some dorms actively recruit certain ethnic groups and genders to bring staff balance, but also as a treatment tool for residents. The idea is that some staff are able to effect certain residents better than others. Females play a significant role at Opportunity Boys' Home; as of August 1988, there were three female social workers and nine females staff persons, totaling 12 of 32 or 37 percent (of the overall dorm staff). Interestingly, of the four main administrators, two are female (one Black, the other White).

Social workers are required to develop treatment plans for residents. Their caseload consists of the residents within their dorm, although at times they are asked to counsel residents from other dorms. Social workers are further expected to write behavioral contracts, termination explanations and graduation summaries. They are primary therapists within dorms, conducting family conferences, individual counseling sessions, probation officers conferences and group counseling. To a lesser degree, other dorm staff (dorm coordinator, case aides counselors, e.g., subordinate staff), perform group and individual counseling, issue penalties, and interact with probation officers. As a rule, subordinate staff do not write treatment plans, terminations explanations or graduation summaries. The most significant writing done by subordinate staff is logging. There is a "daily dorm log" which subordinate staff records routine and unusual activities; e.g., the dorm's dinner behavior, a fight, an ill resident, residents attending outings. Logging functions as a record keeping device and communication network among staff. Subordinate staff also complete incident reports, and awol reports.

Among dorm hierarchy, dorm coordinators are second in command. Coordinators are specifically responsible for staff schedules and identifying tasks for case aides and counselors. Coordinators however do perform many duties of counselors and case aides. For example, counselors and case aides are in large measure social control agents; they have most social contact with residents, and are responsible for making certain that residents carry out their daily routines. They chaperon and accompany residents on outings, transport them to hospitals, juvenile halls, home and even to the airport. The only real difference between case aides and counselors is that case aides tend to have higher degrees (B.A. or M.A.) and earn slightly more money, translating into a higher status.

Given OBH is a 24 hour operation, there is a night staff that arrives after the final evening shift. The evening shift ends at 10pm (Sun-Thurs) and night staff arrives at 9:30pm, working until 6am. On Friday and Saturday, the late shift terminates at 12 midnight and night staff clocks-in at 11pm, working until 7:00am. Night staff have minimal interaction with residents, given their working hours. Structurally, one night staff is assigned to a single dorm, and must be available to residents (if necessary). Night employees are not counselors and are not expected to counsel, albeit many do counsel residents. Essentially, night staff are required to document any residential movement during the night (going to restroom, etc), complaints of illness, check rooms each half hour, and wake kitchen crew residents. Night staff do not wake the remaining residents, for they are wakened by their morning staff (at 6:00am). Finally, if the day staff arrives late, night staff must monitor (cover) that dorm until a replacement arrives. In this case, night employees would perform the routine morning functions of day staff.

Summary

This chapter describes and examines the setting of Opportunity Boys' Home (OBH). It is a community-based treatment facility that counsels juvenile offenders. The idea of residential treatment is to reduce institutionalization; hence the structure of this facility is much different than juvenile hall or youth authority. As a community-based home, OBH is more open and attempts to change delinquent tendencies in youth. Conversely, juvenile hall is closed (locked-down), having very little interest in treatment. Residential treatment programs refer to their clients as residents, not inmates or minors; and such programs are located in various communities so that residents might integrate, having less difficulty returning to mainstream society.

OBH residential staff are referred to in treatment terms, e.g., counselors, social workers, dorm coordinators. They are to provide an environment that is conducive for treatment. This often means making certain that control and order exist; in short, it is difficult to treat chaotic residents. The staff then, work in the five dorms (V, W, X, Y and Z) located at OBH; but more importantly, client dwellings are referred as dorms, not units or cells. This language, or labeling, gets at the community-based nature of OBH.

While dorm life is to reflect "home environment," the school, gym, recreation room, chapel, playing field, laundry room and kitchen are designed to keep residents on campus. There is little reason for residents to leave, given their needs and wants are supplied by OBH. Still, many residents earn off-campus trips to theaters, amusement parks, stores, etc.

Notes

1. The basic treatment philosophy of Opportunity Boys' Home is behavior modification. It is a stimulus response approach in that residents are rewarded for good/appropriate behavior, and punished for deviant behavior.

2. Note that certain residents have written and signed their own passes, and staff may only discover such action if they are searching for the resident.

3. The business director provides the fourth main administrator. I will not discuss his position because his primary role is to manage the business affairs of the Home. He has no regular involvement in control and treatment activities.

4. The O.D. office is approximately ten feet from Henry Nash's office. When both office doors are open, one can hear conversations coming from either office.

Chapter 3

Learning Control

Social control makes up one major feature of staff work at Opportunity Boys' Home. This work consists of counseling residents, monitoring dorms, enforcing institutional rules, breaking up fights, issuing sanctions, negotiating with residents, bedding-down residents, conducting group, etc. How do new-staff learn control at Opportunity Boys' Home (OBH)? And how do experienced-staff learn control during unfamiliar situations? Essentially, learning control is learning the role and work of staff.

When formal training, namely in-service training, is offered, all new staff are required to attend each session. The purpose is to teach new staff how OBH operates. Staff may learn social control without participating in in-service training at OBH, e.g., previous placement experience. Consequently, there are times when various staff have not engaged in formal in-service training, which has led to mistakes in their job performance. In a working class environment, such as OBH, staff are held responsible for their errors. The issue of how blame is accessed becomes significant in order to correct and reduce mistakes; in addition to sanctioning staff so that others are cognizant of the cost of errors. And finally, administrators are able to say: "we've dealt with and documented errors and problems of X-staff."

So then, who's blamed for the mistakes of new staff? New staff? Or those responsible for teaching them? If in-service training covered awoling, and a staff asked a resident to accompany him to retrieve an awolee (which he shouldn't), then the staff is at fault. Staff, on the other hand, would be less guilty had in-service training failed to cover awoling. Again, in-service training becomes significant regarding knowledge of OBH and blame assessment. Moveover, the likelihood of facing unfamiliar situations may be reduced by attending in-service training. Given an unfamiliar situation, staff might stretch a solution or develop a remedy through his or her participation in in-service (formal) training. In short, in-service training could supply ideas and better equip staff on how to manage unforeseen troubles.

We will see, during the course of this chapter, that administrators do not look very kindly on mistakes. While mistakes clearly contribute to learning, administrators would much rather blame staff, than accepting responsibility for new staff and senior staff mistakes. Blaming staff, places administrators in a stronger control position (over staff). Accepting blame, places administrators in an awkward position, making them appear less competent and even vulnerable. Hence, whenever there is blame to assess, it tends to tickle down to new staff and/or experienced staff.

Formal Training

New staff and experienced staff learned control by formal training, observing other staff, making mistakes, and assistance from residents. While each category is examined, formal training involves in-service training, Professional Assaultive Restraint Training (or PART), university education and conferences related to social work, as a type of formal, theoretical training.

New line staff usually receive in-service training,[1] which occurs once weekly for ten weeks. During in-service training, new staff work in their assigned dorm, attempting to practice what they are learning. The specific function of in-service training is to officially teach new staff how OBH operates and appropriate control behaviors and strategies of staff towards residents. In-service training is taught by Intake Worker Inga Haynes, who is an authoritarian African American female. During in-service training Inga focuses on issues and procedures that new staff are likely to encounter. For instance, how to write incident reports (which are formal reports of resident wrongdoings and facility damage); how to report and write-up awols, e.g., residents leaving OBH without permission; how to respond to panic buttons (OBH emergencies); restraining residents when too aggressive, procedures on walking residents to school, laundry procedures, kitchen regulations, expectations of staff during meals, function of the

Officer of the Day (OD) and when to contact O.D.s; how to report child abuse, manage complaints from residents; how to log (or document) properly, signing one's name in and out of the main log, clocking in and out; how to use a resident's medical packet (which contains medical information in case of emergency); procedures on transporting residents to juvenile hall, home, hospital and outings. New employees are over-whelmed with information during these sessions. Many staff admit that they do not grasp all the "facts" and details conveyed in training sessions. And given the "freshness" of new employees, it is questionable whether they process all such materials and information.

At times, Inga invites certain personnel (laundry supervisor, kitchen supervisor, night supervisor, etc) to discuss their department, and entertain questions from new line staff. While supervisors seemed informative and Inga's seminars appeared useful, several problems emerged from in-service sessions. For example, staff complained that issues were raised though never solved or clarified. That is, resident awols would be the primary topic, and somehow the discussion diverted to juvenile hall, then to restraining residents, and never returning to the original subject, awoling. Other staff complained that in-service was too theoretical, that sessions were cancelled and not rescheduled, that ten-week-training-sessions were never completed; and that some new staff never received in-service train-ing.

New counselor, Carl Pete believes that new personnel receive plenty of information. But the key is how such knowledge is "executed." He states:

> "They tell you allot, but you have to execute it, use your own discretion. Allot of these staff are not used to kids jumping in their face...The weak staff will listen to that stuff (information given in orientation), but they are afraid to confront these kids."[2]

To what extent are new staff capable of "executing" their assignments outside the presence of senior staff? When a resident is "jumping in their (staff's) face," how do new staff respond? Handle it alone or seek help from senior staff? Orientation is useful but orientation cannot break up a fight, confront residents or prevent residents from "jumping in [your] face." Carl believes that new staff are not accustom to such behavior, and while "weak staff" are receptive to in-service training, "they are afraid to confront these kids." In short, weak staff who are new, seem unable to "execute" their assignments regardless of information volume. More generally, staff complaints concerning in-service training raises questions about its effectiveness.

In some cases, several months passed before Inga scheduled in-service training for new staff. In-service training, oftentimes, was prompted by the amount of new staff who were unaware of OBH forms and procedures, leading to several problems regarding how to control residents and consistency concerning procedures.

Portions of formalized training include PART instruction, which is a more recent control method at OBH; it was established during the summer of 1988. The object was to teach new and experienced staff how to de-escalate emotional/chaotic situations and proper restraint techniques. All staff working with residents were required to attend the two day, eight hour sessions. On the first day, the theory of PART was explained, and much discussion surfaced from debating theoretical explanations. The second day involved a practical application of the theory, along with being taught and participating in demonstrations of proper restraint methods.

Staff were very opinionated about PART training; one social worker expressed, "the session was helpful in terms of physical restraint techniques, but unless I constantly practice the techniques, I'm bound to forget when I go to restrain a kid or de-escalating a situation." Two female staff (one social work, one line staff) believed that PART was useful, giving them more confidence when an assaultive situation confronted them. Social worker Phil Simmons noticed and verbalized that PART training seemed to increase the amount of staff who pressed the panic button. Finally, social worker Rob Bans, who attended a week long conference to learn PART and actually taught it to OBH staff, was extremely enthusiastic about PART, wanting every staff member to experience PART.

Additionally, Opportunity Boys' Home began videotaping group sessions during the spring of 1989. At the recommendation of the executive director, a "group consultant" was hired to formally teach staff how to become better group leaders. The idea, according the group consultant, was to develop staff into better, more efficient group leaders. That is, group leaders who could facilitate and get more out of residents involved in group. Thus, group sessions were videotaped and later the consultant along with staff reviewed the taped group session, pointing out problems and how staff could improved group skills, control skills and encouraging staff where proficient.

Formal education is another method by which many staff learn social work and social control. The University provides theoretical explanations for social behavior in coercive institutions (Etzioni, 1975). Oftentimes, theories are discussed and debated, allowing professors and students (in some cases) to arrive at consensus on social problems, and possibly develop solutions. Those students who eventually work in coercive institutions and have not entered the field are often shocked at what they learn and experience when placed in the field. Indeed, most OBH staff possess university degrees and new staff often confess, "you can never learn this (treatment) from the books," recognizing the gap between university education and practical applications. The University can inform students about the problem. However, within the confines of the classroom, the university cannot help students and potential staff experience problems in coercive institutions. Most naive and isolated students receive the impression (from the university) that they have experienced, and can therefore solve the problem. While formal university education is beneficial, there is no substitute for practical experience.

Learn by Doing, and Learning Control from Others

Most OBH employees believe that they receive little on the job training and required to manage a dorm before ready. At some juncture, every staff must oversee a dorm alone, never certain of what to anticipate. Working alone, for the first time, is a very significant learning experience for new staff. It is more or less an "initiation ceremony" (Goffman, 1961) in that staff are frequently challenged by residents. The first time out, staff might experience residents fighting, sniffing paint, smoking in their rooms, or a resident cursing staff. In each case, the staff may learn from his handling of the situation, becoming more comfortable and relaxed with his position.[3]

Winny's first days at OBH seemed overwhelming. As she entered the O.D. office to clock out and sign out, we greeted one another and I asked, "How are things goin'?" She placed her bags on the couch, signed out and confessed, "I was about to walk out of here about a week ago." "Why!?" I asked. "Because I felt like I had a work overload, and I felt more like a policewoman rather than a therapist." I agreed, sympathizing, "Yeeesss, when you first start here, you receive lots and lots of information that you can't possibly remember, but during the course of training..." Winny interrupted and disagreed by raising her voice, exclaiming, "TRAINING!!? WHAT TRAINING!!??" We both laughed. Then she continued, "this has been nothing but O-J-T (on the job training) from day one."

Winny does not literally mean on the job training, for in the traditional sense, on the job training suggests that the employer formally trains, demonstrates and teaches employees while working (Altonji & Spletzer, 1991). When Winny disputes my claim to training, she is arguing that she has received no training and thereby placed in a situation to learn by doing, or "on the job learning."

This is not uncommon for staff to learn their role by doing their job; the only way one can experience control is by doing control. For example, how does one learn bed-down procedure? In many cases, staff walk up and down the dorm corridor telling residents to "bed-down" or "go to bed". Staff check rooms making sure residents are preparing for bed, or in bed, and handle resident requests, like, "I need a sheet." Thus, in the process of doing (and observing other staff while "doing"), staff learn which requests to honor and which to deny; residents who are postponing and abusing bedtime and residents who are not; and therefore, when to issue a "night problem" and when to overlook such problems. Night-problems are characterized as rule violations and defiance to staff by residents, during bedtime. Defiant residents intentionally disturb other residents from sleeping and staff from attending to other nightly assignments, e.g., dorm logging, incident report writing, confirming home passes, etc. X-dorm places the heaviest emphasis on night problems because they may disrupt the entire dorm, affect the morning routine and environment, and/or spillover into other dorms and departments. In short, staff learn the bed-down structure by simultaneously watching and doing.

Staff also learn how to process purchase orders (POs) by doing them. Purchase orders are fifty to $100 dollar clothing stipends that residents receive from the Probation department, upon entry into OBH. OBH has an account with J.C. Penney in order to transact purchase orders. Processing purchase orders is often discussed in in-service training, in addition to senior staff explaining to new staff how to process purchase orders. If staffing permits there are times when new staff accompany senior staff on purchase orders. But it is more common for new staff to receive instructions, then do the purchase order.

While purchase orders involve transporting residents to J.C. Penney, new staff learn several "things" when doing purchase orders. First, residents who have purchase orders are anxious about shopping. When Dave, from Z-dorm, informs certain residents (in his dorm) that he will take them on a purchase order after dinner, it is often the case that residents excitedly talk about what they will purchase. Through hearing residents talk about purchase orders, it is also likely that residents from other dorms who have purchase orders will inquire whether they too can attend the purchase order outing.

Second, new staff learn that processing purchase orders "take a long time." That is, residents often look at clothing throughout the store; they look at store items other than clothing; and, the process of trying on and fitting clothing may be very lengthy. Staff must be available to examine clothing choices and purchases of residents, for staff must guard against the selection and purchase of gang clothing. Lastly then, staff learn that they must engage in a type of "clothing control" while shopping. That is, control of the type of clothing purchased and control of possible shoplifting by residents. After doing purchase orders, many staff express dismay for purchase orders because of the above process and problems. And while purchase orders are fun and exciting for residents, they become headaches for staff.[4]

While doing control, some new staff experience a type of degradation ceremony when confronting residents. X-dorm counselor, Stephanie, was only following procedure when she asked Evans (resident) to fill in the X-dorm dining area. That is, a dorms' dining area must be filled before residents are permitted to sit in another area. Consider the following exchange:

> The only open seat in X-dorm section was by Stephanie. When Stephanie noticed that Evans was seating himself next to Rose (in the Z-dorm section), she instructed Evans to, "fill up the X-dorm section first before you sit over there." In a loud voice unconcerned about Stephanie's feelings, Evans blurted, "I sure as hell ain't gonna sit over there if I have to sit by you!" Evans continued eating as if Stephanie did not exist. Stephanie did not press the issue, nor respond in kind; she simply guided her attention elsewhere. ...She wanted to hide in a shell, or so it appeared.

My description of Stephanie wanting "to hide in a shell," implies a certain embarrassment and incidental learning. Apparently, Stephanie did not respond for fear of another outburst by Evans. She did however learn that Evans was not shy about openly expressing his feelings. It is possible that her next similar encounter with Evans (or some other resident) will be different, in that Stephanie must learn alternative approaches of control and controlling Evans. Additionally, Stephanie's embarrassing moment may have resulted from my observation of the entire event. That is, after the embarrassing outburst, our eyes briefly touched, and she immediately focused her attention elsewhere.

Learning control by observing other staff is assumed and quite natural for new staff (See Jerold Heiss, 1981 & Viktor Gecas,1981). New staff are not expected to "jump in and take over," but they are advised to watch, ask questions and learn from experienced staff. Some staff take longer to acquire an independent control style (Black,1984), but observation of others and ones own ability helps new staff in developing a control style. Alisse acknowledged that while she observes senior staff, she further acquired a preference for working with certain senior staff. That is, Alisse enjoys working with "Big Sal" because she has gained a respect for Sal's control ability, believing she can learn much from him (an experienced staff). On the other hand, Alisse recognizes that other staff are not as astute as they think, thereby having "much more to learn." As in any work environment, new staff at OBH acquire a preference regarding who they want to work with and learn from.

Further, certain new staff appear more passive when observing situational encounters between staff and residents. For instance, new staff observe experienced staff during group sessions (with residents), during panic button responses, during conferences with parents and probation officers, during school & kitchen line-ups. The idea is to learn how to process group or respond to a panic button, to assist where needed but not take over. New staff, Diane, was passively observed in group watching how Sal and Tye conducted group with residents; "she was quiet and appeared as though she was trying to learn OBH group techniques." Maria was observed standing in the hallway watching experienced staff respond to a panic button. In a conversation with Andrea, she expressed a joy in working at OBH, yet admitted: "I'm still learning. But what I do is watch other senior staff, or at least senior to me, and see how they handle situations and I pick up certain things from them."

When working a dorm alone, there is a support system for new staff throughout OBH. That is, if a problem occurs new staff may consult with staff from other dorms, seek advice from Officer of the Day (who is in charge of OBH and manages the Home after administrative staff leaves) or call the home of an off duty co-worker. In the case of Melisia, new staff, she was confused over whether she should write an incident report regarding a broken window in W-dorm. She consulted the O.D. and he advised her to "write the incident report." Evita, also new staff, was unsure of what action to take when residents severely act out. Thus, as Evan (staff) strolled through the hallway, she stopped him for advice. Evan explains: "O.K., I was walking down to Z-dorm to get my guys for the basketball game. I saw Evita and she told me that Coville (resident) was being destructive, by throwing chairs, trashcans and books on the floor. She asked me what should she do, and I told her to write it up, so that it would be dealt with properly tomorrow in group."

Reggie was a new staff who observed experienced staff, asked questions and seemingly learned from his observation. He conveyed an incident that disturbed him, yet was impressed by the handling of the confrontation, gaining a certain respect for the staff in action:

> "While we (X-dorm residents) were in the dinner line, our line was noisy and so was hers (the residents of Mickee's Y-dorm line). She took her guys back to the dorm, and because I'm kinda new, I asked her if I could take mine back. She said 'yes', so I took them back. When I told them to go back to the dorm, Garcia said, 'you gonna listen to that hoe?' Mickee handled it pretty good. At first, she came at him pretty strong, but Garcia still had his chest stuck out; you know, he was trying to act big in front of the guys. Then she used reverse psychology on him. She said, 'I'm really disappointed in you. I thought you were better than that.' Then Garcia kinda put his head down, but he was listenin'!" According to Reggie, Mickee requested that he (Garcia) write her a composition, and be put "on hold" (loss of privileges for three days). Reggie then said: "They even shook hands afterwards, and Mickee offered to help him write the composition, if he needed help."

In this case, Reggie learned that there are alternative ways of confronting residents. If one particular strategies is not working, changing to less intimidating methods may obtain desired results.

Learning by observation and conversation is not uncommon in the O.D. office. It is a place where staff sign-in and out of the main log and clock-in and out. Conversation often occurs among staff who have arrived early, and await the proper time to clock-in or out. While conversation may range from the days' events to some external occurrence, there is usually some mention of the time clock and Jan Waner (personnel director in charge of payroll). Manual and Rog, V-dorm counselors, entered the O.D. office, noticed Dorie (attractive, new female staff) and introduced themselves. After Manual shook her hand, he sat directly across from her and began advising this new staff. Relaxing back with his legs crossed, Manual explained, "The first thing you gotta learn about the time clock is that if you don't want a note from Jan, clock-out right here (rises to point where she must clock out) at ten o'clock." Then Dorie nodded with a shy smile saying, "O.K." It follows that staff not only learn residential control issues, but how to control and prevent annoying notes from the Personnel director.

In large measure, learning control occurs by observing other staff. Staff tend to ask questions, seek assistance, advice and information from experienced staff. In turn, senior staff willingly provide information to new staff, and explanations for their actions. Since encounters are never the same at Opportunity Boys' Home, new staff receive a "frame" (Goffman, 1974) of how to interpret and handle recurring events. Learning by doing and observing other staff is a type of informal training for new staff. Here staff learn what is not taught in formal in-service training, e.g., how to "tailor" incident reports, how to negotiate with residents, how to handle tests, how to handle embarrassment and how to forcefully restrain residents. And given the informal nature of this learning, senior staff who taught and advised new staff are not necessarily held accountable.

Learning by Mistake

> "But you know the way people learn things around
> here is by making mistakes. You make a mistake
> around here and boooy they'll be in your shit."

At OBH, one of the most severe ways of learning is by making mistakes. Certain errors become a major source of trouble for line staff in relation to administration. For instance, staff buying cigarettes for residents, staff stealing money from residents and/or staff fighting residents amounts to major sources of trouble. The outcome of "trouble" is some type of sanction, for instance, a write-up, suspension, firing, scolding or conference with administration. Intentional errors undermine formal norms and organizational structure of OBH, not to mention citations by State Licensing. Unintentional mistakes by novice staff produces a temporary tolerance though blame is still assessed. In either case, certain staff mistakes could prompt external evaluation, causing Licensing to be more cognizant of OBH, e.g., external trouble, and possibly changing external perceptions and relations with OBH.

New staff Cosy was involved in a major violation by permitting two residents to assist him in taking Franks (resident) to juvenile hall. This action is contrary to OBH policy in that co-workers, not residents, are to assist one another in transporting residents to juvenile hall. Apparently, the experienced staff was either unaware of the policy or Cosy and Mickee had very poor communication, for Mickee (experienced staff) gave permission. An error in communication does seem plausible given the chaotic nature of Y-dorm. According to Cosy, "it was crazy down there (Y-dorm). We were running around, and I asked Mickee if it was alright (to take two residents, in an OBH van, searching for Franks who had awoled) and she said 'yeah', so I went on. Then when I caught up with Franks, I called and Marra said it was alright too, so I went on (to juvenile hall, with Franks and two assisting residents)."

As a new employee and during a chaotic dorm situation, Cosy was simply working hard, trying to "do the right thing." Yet, "when I (Cosy) got back, I had to hear it from Nash and Janette!" That is, he was sanctioned by the executive director and clinical director, respectively.[5] Humorously recapping his juvenile hall scenario, Cosy appeared rather embarrassed, realizing, "I guess we learn by our mistakes." Though Cosy was not completely at fault, he was victimized by poor communication and a chaotic dorm (or possibly the lack of knowledge by senior staff), and received most of the sting. Consequently, one latent function of making mistakes is learning that residents should not assist or accompany staff when transporting minors to Juvenile Hall. Moreover, staff learn that they are "in trouble" with administration. After conferencing with administration, staff learn how to control residents in ways more acceptable by administration.

Finally, some senior staff, who are responsible for training new staff, maintain that new staff must learn by "trial and error." While relaxing in the O.D. office and leaving a new staff to cover X-dorm, Tye and I heard a loud confrontation between new staff and various residents. Senior staff, Tye, expressed, "Yeah, gotta break him in. See man, this is something you can't teach. You gotta learn by trial and error." In other words, experienced staff cannot and should not rescue or "hold the hand" of new staff constantly. New staff should have opportunities to encounter residents and conduct groups in order to learn and enact their roles. There is a certain status gained or lost in ones ability to perform their roles, independently of senior staff.

In sum, mistakes are clearly learning devices; staff learn their roles, e.g., specific "dos and don'ts," and that certain mistakes creates troubles for staff. When mistakes result in trouble, administration focuses-in on the responsible party (or parties), assessing blame where appropriate. Identifying responsible parties helps administrators control staff population. There is a type of anxiety built into meeting in the offices of administrators when one knows he is in "trouble." Staff are uncertain of outcomes, though administrators are interested in finding out facts, then assessing blame and sanction. Many staff who make unintentional errors are often sorry, wishing that the incident never occurred, but somehow, they are still made to feel incompetent by administration, e.g., "you can work really hard but when you make a mistake, they really come down on you." Most staff recognize the type of power administration possesses and in large measure, this power is used to keep staff in "check" (in control). If staff make too many unintentional errors, administration may perceive them as liabilities, therefore opting to terminate. The working class reality here is "shape up or ship out," for too many mistakes become grounds for dismissal or some other sanction.

Learning Control From Residents

Lewis Coser (1990) and James Jacobs (1977) contend that subordinates and superiors in total institutions and organizational environments are dependent on one another. Coser (1990) argues that camp guards could not have controlled the numerous inmates without assistance from inmates. Jacobs (1977) found that inmates at Stateville achieved higher statuses in exchange for overseeing other inmates, e.g., monitor work assignments and completion of tasks. And Van Deburg (1987) illustrates how planters relied on slave drivers to manage and oversee their property. At Opportunity Boys' Home staff and residents are similarly dependent on one another for social control as well as learning.

Learning takes on an interesting twist when new staff learn from residents. That is, there is a type of direct learning, when staff ask residents formal questions; a type of learning assistance, when residents sit with staff volunteering information. And lastly, residents testing staff result in learning for staff.

There seems to be a link between new staff and residents testing staff. More often than not, new staff are tested by residents to determine new staff limits, strengths, and weaknesses. The test of one resident (or a group of residents) functions as a socializer for other residents and staff. The initial "initiation" of staff by residents, and the handling of the encounter by staff, gives residents an indication of the type of staff controlling them.

Alternatively, "initiation ceremonies" by residents functions to teach new staff the type of incidents that will occur and something about the resident(s) responsible for the incident. Without question, initial tests and confrontations assist new staff in learning control.

New staff have faced beer runs (awoling to the store to buy beer and usually returning to OBH to drink it), on ground awols (OGA), awols, residents cursing staff, fights between residents, contraband (marijuana, weapons) in dorms, intercourse among same sex residents (sex-play) and fights among staff and residents. While all staff experience tests, the act of tests to new staff seem more exciting and amusing to residents. Often, there is no grievance between staff and resident. There is simply the curiosity of how one will act (or react) in a given situation. Alternatively, various staff believe that there are residents who conspire to annoy and test them. Here then new staff are learning from residents and adapting to new situations. In turn, residents are adapting to new staff, new personalities and new ways of working and interacting with residents. However, some new staff become so irritated by resident tests that they temporarily lose control of their reactions. For instance:

> Near the end of her shift (9:50pm), Charoletta called me in the O.D. office and requested that I come down to X-dorm and simply walk through. She felt that my presence would quiet various noisy residents. After residents were settled, Charoletta and I began to talk. She conveyed an incident that occurred between Loza (Chicano resident) and herself in the lobby of the O.D. office. According to Charoletta, the incident occurred after the talent show (8:35pm) as she was returning to X-dorm via O.D. lobby, passing Loza as she walked. "Out of the clear blue," according to Charoletta, "Loza called me a bitch. I rared back and swung at him; had it not been for Lewis (X-dorm resident who was also in the lobby) I may have hit him." Lewis pulled Loza back as Charoletta swung. Charolett said that she was fed up with the disrespect from residents and was not interested in losing her job, for she had planned to resign. Charoletta further said that "the bitch word is getting on my nerves and I lost it when he called me a bitch; I wanted to kill him." "Has he been buggin' you?" I asked. "Yes, when I'm in the office, Loza comes in and hangs around the office. I ask him to leave, but before you know it, he's back again. Then, I ask Jeri (another female staff) to stay in the office while I walk the floor, but then he's following behind me. So he's been trying to get at me all day but tonight I couldn't take it anymore!" confessed Charoletta.

Lary was also provoked by Hill's (resident) command for immediate service. Consider the incident:

> Lary (recreation staff) came to the O.D. office to clock out; he sat in the chair directly across from me, waiting for 9pm. With his New York accent, he expressed very boldly, "Paul, I almost kicked Hill's ass today!" "How did it come about?" I asked. Lary: "O.K., Charoletta and Tellie (staff) were down in the gym because they wanted to buy some sodas. So I was getting them the sodas and Hill (resident) came up, talkin' all loud, saying, 'man, I want to buy a soda.' So I said, 'man you gonna have to wait!' Hill said, 'no man, I want it now!!' So I told Charoletta and Tellie to move out of my way. I came out of the canteen and shut the door, then I said to him, 'Now whats up?' He started pointing his finger in my face (Note: Lary is acting out the scene, e.g., standing and pointing towards his cheek area). Then, when he touched me, I took his hand and 'mushed' him and he fell to the ground.[6] Charoletta and Tellie were grabbin' me and holding me back, but I told them to 'let me go.' So they let me go and I asked him (Hill), 'What you wanna do?' He was about five feet away pointin' and talkin' shit, 'whats up, whats up...' but he knew better. I would have kicked his ass. I told him to leave the gym. He got mad and started throwing things around the gym but that didn't bother me. You know, you can throw shit all you want, but don't put your hands on me."
>
> Lary was extremely disturbed by the incident. After his demonstration, he again sat in the chair across from me and began to reason, "You can't let these kids push you around. If you let one push you, they'll all be doin' it. I don't let street kids fuck with me. How am I gonna let these kids mess with me? No No!!"

In these two incidents, staff eventually learn to expect testing from residents. They also learn that they cannot predict how they will react. It is clear however that staff should have learned the appropriate circumstance regarding how to restrain and respond to residents. Through interaction and situational conditions, staff and residents learn the limits of staff, that is, just how much staff will take before reacting in kind. Moreover, staff learn that control procedures endorsed by OBH and taught to staff may not be enough to control residents and minimize tests. Certain encounters find staff being overly aggressive; but apparently, staff feel vindicated by their actions, recognizing that routine procedures don't work. Like policemen who informally abuse citizens, staff also "teach them (residents) a lesson," designed to ease future encounters. Consequently, staff learn from testing, gaining experience in how to manage future tests.[7]

Experienced staff recognize that new staff are tested and challenged more often. Tye (X-dorm counselor) acknowledged that "residents see new staff as 'new booty' and there is open game on them. They (residents) try to get away with anything." Winna, on the other hand, assumed that her initiation would be short, and soon discovered otherwise. She states, "You know when I got here I knew I would be tested. I thought 'oh this'll go on for about a week and everything will be alright.' But I don't think so." This suggest that the duration and type of tests experienced by new staff varies according to their ability, previous experience, perceptions residents have of staff, knowledge and stock of knowledge.

Fresh new staff may find themselves at a disadvantage to residents concerning their knowledge of OBH operations. Depending on previous experience and staffing availability, a staff may be thrust into a single handed control situation within a matter of days or weeks. Most residents are more socialized and adjusted to OBH than new staff. For residents, by virtue of their placement, know and understand the operational dorm structure, having been detained longer than the recent hiring of new staff. Consequently, residents are in positions to test new staff and/or "sincerely" assist them.

Those residents who go beyond the call of duty in assisting staff are labeled "junior staff." "Junior staff" is a local term, developed by residents to characterize other residents most likely to "kiss up to staff" and "snitch" on fellow residents. "Junior staff" are often seen with staff, helping new staff, believing and supporting OBH program, and viewed as "staff's pet." Given this derogatory label and achieved status, "junior staff" are harassed by residents who considered them "pests" and "snitches". Resident interpretation of "junior staff" is very significant because many residents view staff as members of the out-group. In the minds of some residents, it is a clear case of "us against them." The "junior staff" then, has selected a risky alternative, which could ostracize him from other residents.

Yet, "junior staff" seem available to new staff when they (new staff) must conduct group, monitor kitchen behavior and enforce dorm closure for the first few times, e.g., when "junior staff" are needed. New staff who are in these situations are sometimes reluctant to accept the information and counsel of "junior staff," for new staff question the credibility of such advice. If the "junior staff's" information proves reliable, new staff may come to depend on "junior staff" as a source of knowledge, which may evolve further into an informal and formal exchange relationship. That is, in exchange for knowledge and advice, new staff might formally or informally reward "junior staff" with extra privileges or a high dorm status.

Even new staff acknowledge that "junior staff" are valuable with very simple procedural and situational issues. For example, when a senior staff clock out, leaving new staff on duty alone, new staff are often confronted with residential requests (requests that residents often know the answer). For example, a resident requesting to keep on his night light because he is restless and wishes to continue reading and writing (after bedtime hours), may seem harmless to new staff. This is prohibited because all dorm room lights should be out before night staff reports on duty, at 9:30pm. The rule guards against deviant behavior that is probable. OBH believes that additional reading and writing might occur during quiet hour (also referred to as "study hour"), during school or any other part of the day when residents have free time. New staff who view the request as reasonable, may consult "junior staff," receiving the "proper" information. Now staff can use this information as he sees fit.

The credibility of "junior staff" information is established through time. The rightness or wrongness of information is uncovered with each event. Generally, "junior staff" are liked by most staff and sometimes residents. In fact, staff come to depend on them to "be their eyes" while they're temporarily away, run errands, help break-up fights and act as dorm monitor (who monitors residents during study hour, line-ups and distributes snacks to residents). Junior staff make themselves known to administration, who often praise their behavior, citing the exemplary quality of such behavior, wishing more residents were like "them". More often then not, junior staff generally receive the covenant award of "boy of the month," which includes being displayed during an informal ceremony of Opportunity Club members, receiving a plaque and spending money. New staff, senior staff and administrators benefit and learn from credible "junior staff." For staff, "junior staff" are in many ways like having an assistant.

One does not have to be a "junior staff" to assist new staff in learning control. Andrea mentioned that she not only liked her job but enjoyed working with the boys. She said, "the boys are nice to me; sometimes when they see me doing something wrong, they correct me and tell me the right way." Another case in point is Dorie, who draws much attention from residents and male staff because of her beauty. Dorie seems to use her beauty to "break the ice" with residents thus acquiring possible informants.

It is common however to observe residents rushing to sit by and around Dorie during meals. In the course of dinner conversation, residents assist her by routinely identifying problematic residents and how to manage problems and procedures in the dorm.

Discussion

This chapter explores how staff learn control; it is a process that occurs through several different strategies, in that, staff learn through formal training, observations, mistakes, resident testing and resident assistance. This chapter further reveals that distinct learning styles and situations are significant to "completely" and "efficiently" learning one's role, particularly those issues that go un-addressed. Consequently, informal learning (observing other staff, mistakes and learning from residents) and its practice may very well prove the difference between "sinking or swimming," or being labeled weak or strong. Some staff grasped their roles better by observing other staff instead of formal training. This begs the question of ones ability to execute what is formally learned. On the job learning seems valuable to new staff, yet there are costs and benefits. That is, there is always the possibility of error, which could lead to conflict and trouble; but there's the possibility of heroism, thus achieving a status of respect and admiration among fellow staff and residents. The real issue is learning control (or learning ones role), and how to function in this coercive environment. Upon entry then, learning is not only immediate but ongoing; and new staff working with specific senior staff are frequently influenced by the particular work style of experienced staff. Still, the key is developing ones own work style to survive in what can (sometimes) be viewed as a hostile work environment.

Notes

1. New social workers also attended in-service training. In-service training is frequently referred to as new staff orientation.

2. "Jumping in their [your] face" refers to residents who are anxious about receiving attention or finding out about a staff decision (home passes, outings, dorm closures, holds) that will effect them (or him). Such anxiety may lead

residents to constantly bother staff, to the point of irritation and even disrespect. "Jumping in your face" may further result from residents receiving sanctions (penalties that disturb them), and/or "not getting their way." The resident who jumps in the face of staff becomes a pain, an irritant to staff.

3. See Jerold Heiss, "Social Roles," 1981, and Albert Bandura, *Social Learning Theory*, 1977 for a critical analysis of how social roles are learned.

4. Note that when staff-A from V-dorm discovers that staff-B from Z-dorm is processing purchase orders, staff-A is likely to inquire whether staff-B can process additional purchase orders (from his dorm), and whether staff-B will permit certain residents to attend. Staff would rather put purchase orders off on someone else (some other staff).

5. Evan (Z-dorm, dorm coordinator) shares the sentiments of Perry and Cosy, commenting: "it seems that you learn by making mistakes; you can work really hard but when you make a mistake they really come down on you." That is, administration "comes down on" staff.

6. Mushed: Covering Hill's face with the palm of his hand and pushing him.

7. In Lary's case, the intake director was informed of the incident by V-dorm staff (Randy). The director meant with Lary to receive his version; in turn, Lary received a verbal warning. Hill (resident) was also counseled by the intake director, V-dorm staff and myself because of his apparent intent to "equal the score" by hitting Gary with a belt and stick.

Chapter 4

Everyday Control

This chapter examines how staff in a juvenile detention center experience and respond to everyday rule violations by residents. Staff responses to resident rule violations may vary from ignoring, to dirty looks, to bargaining, to on-the-spot correction (without sanction), to write-ups, to punishing residents in a variety of ways. Staff reaction to resident wrongdoing is largely based on staff perception. At the heart of this process is staff's constant concern with maintaining control.

Theoretically, I am concerned with how order is maintained by doing control in everyday circumstances. This theoretical concentration gets at the process of maintaining order and control within OBH institutional structure. Order is created and maintained daily; formal rules help to structure behavior and staff/resident interactions, but rules and order are often negotiated. Staff are charged with enforcing rules and with control more broadly, but exactly how is this done?

There is a clear difference, however, between managing order and enforcing rules. That is, managing order may not require staff to enforce rules. Staff may look the other way when rule violations seem harmless. Or gesturally, staff may make their presence known to deter certain inappropriate actions. Enforcing rules, conversely, requires that staff take some type of formal action, e.g., insisting that residents line-up before meals or turning off the T.V. during quiet hour (also referred as study hour).

Order and rules are negotiated in another sense: they are frequently challenged by residents, and must be upheld and actively enforced by staff. Thus, through staff responses to rule infractions, we begin to see how order is created and maintained daily. Order does not simply exist; thus the question of how order is maintained through doing control is the major theme of this chapter.

How staff do everyday control shapes the overall "feel" and atmosphere of the Home. That is, while staff are required to maintained control, such maintenance gives residents and staff a feeling of stability and security. Residents believe that their troubles and problems will be addressed, and staff work at higher comfort and security levels. Clearly, Opportunity Boys' Home does not provide a "home" or "family" atmosphere for residents, yet consistent and everyday control by staff influences attitudes and the overall OBH structure.

I have identified two categories of staff control responses: situational remedies and institutional responses. Situational remedies include staff efforts to control situations with resources personally available to them; this usually involves correcting a resident's wrongdoing immediately and often without sanction. Moreover, other outside staff are typically not informed or involved. Institutional remedies are linked to more serious rule violations which are handled through formal institutional procedures (incident reports, documentation in dorm and main logs, counseling-group sessions, informing other staff, school incident reports) and agents outside the situation. Compared to situational remedies, institutional responses require more investigative work and frequently result in some sort of formal punishment.

The use of these responses, in specific situations, requires skill and knowledge on the part of staff. Staff should be able to interpret and handle minor violations without assistance; thus recognizing that if violations were ignored, they would cause little or no harm. Regarding {more} serious institutional violations, staff should also possess a skill and knowledge of how to handle such infractions. That is, at what point are other staff requested? How are infractions handled? What is the appropriate documentation and sanction for the incident? Here staff must learn a proper balance of the two, i.e., staff who make too frequent use of institutional responses, or who are seen to do so inappropriately, are viewed as unable to effectively maintain control. Alternatively, staff who make frequent use of situational remedies are viewed as strong, intelligent and independent control agents. However, whether one should independently handle residents who are "out of control" is questionable. Consequently, a changing of perception by other staff could emerge resulting from one's failure to seek assistance. Finally, staff should know when to terminate a resident who is housed in open placement. That is, having exhausted all possibilities to modify delinquent tendencies, this is key a indicator that a particular resident "doesn't belong here."

While the proposed aim of the institution is primarily treatment, it is difficult to modify behavior unless staff receives cooperation from residents. An implied assumption in staff responses to rule violations is not only restoring order but managing behavior. That is, it is unwise for staff to sanction every infraction; indeed, it is difficult and troublesome to identify each offense. Some infractions go unsanctioned while other violations are hardly penalized as an informal trade off for "good behavior." Here then, staff are wedded to their own situational dilemma, e.g., at which point and in what situations should sanctions be negotiated and/or administered? This becomes a very delicate situation for staff, because residents constantly observe staff/resident interaction and decisions, expecting similar treatments in similar circumstances.

Situational Remedies

OBH staff engage in various types of routine work daily: Lining residents up for school and dinner; bedding-down residents and making sure their lights are off; monitoring quiet hour--where residents are in their rooms for an hour each weekday. During quiet hour, residents occupy themselves by studying, writing letters, reading, etc. There is quiet talk among roommates, but listening to radios, even quietly, is absolutely prohibited. Moreover, conducting group becomes routine in that it is held daily. Groups are held for informative and issue-oriented purposes. Of all their tasks, perhaps the above types of routine work are easiest to learn and apply; still, it is within this everyday "frame" that trivial and serious violations occur. It is a routine and structure that functions to stabilize the everyday operation of OBH, and it is the most accessible mechanism by which new staff learn. Access to this "routine environment" enables staff to develop skills and form judgements about varying situations.

Consider, for example, resident line-ups at OBH: lining up for meals occurs three times daily; lining up for school happens twice a day. If, for example, a staff member judges a line to be crooked, he might refuse to proceed until the line is straight; someone else might simply ignore the line entirely, believing that crooked lines have no bearing on behavior. Though differences of interpretation exist among counselors, staff possess authority to judge situations as they see them, effecting how order is viewed and maintained.

The following cases guide us through a process of situational remedies, e.g., how staff perceive and respond to minor rule violations by residents. It is a process experienced by staff in that they define situations, determine violations and determine how violations are handled. Furthermore, staff situational responses to troubles are often spontaneous, and in some cases reactive. This reflects a wide and creative range of social control options and styles (available to staff), as well as the situational nature of the encounter.

The notion of "everyday control" implies that staff engage in control oriented behavior daily. Their job is to maintain order and stability in a facility where some residents regularly break rules. Maintaining order involves constant decision making; and given the nature of people work, staff often chose simple and innovative ways to handle trivial rule infractions. Staff regularly employ a variety of situational and spontaneous strategies to control minor problems. These include "ordering," "snatching," "yelling and grabbing," and "requesting." Each is analyzed in its own context as instances of how staff actually manage what they view as situational responses.

Ordering

Ordering involves staff giving an authoritative command to residents to correct rule infractions instantly. The following case examines the kitchen supervisor who observes a resident taking a milk during a time not permitted, "seconds." She orders him to "put it back!!" Consider this scenario:

> Midway through dinner, as I stood behind the food counter, I observed Wynn (Z-dorm resident) holding Z-dorm snack box while looking at and picking up a "staff milk,"[1] located near the salads. Wynn nonchalantly picked up the milk as myself and Misty (kitchen director) stood observing him from different angles. I was behind the food counter (at the end of the food line). Misty stood at the end of the food counter, next to the milk crate

for residents, near the food-line exit door. Wynn was very noticeable because "seconds" were being served and few residents were returning for "seconds". So, as Wynn drew closer to us, he naturally caught our attention. Initially, when he picked up the "staff milk," no one said anything, and its interesting to note that Wynn casually picked up the milk as if we were not there and as if he was doing nothing wrong. I had no intention of confronting Wynn, but once he had a firm grip on the milk, Misty scolded, "put that milk back!!" Wynn looked up in surprise and Misty repeated, "put it back!!" Wynn questioned, "Why? I didn't get a milk when I first went through; I had a coke." Misty was not concerned about his excuse, she simply wanted him to return the milk. As Wynn placed the milk back on ice, Misty then explained, "You can only have one milk. You can't have a milk during 'seconds.'" Wynn walked passed Misty, not really looking at her, saying, "I didn't have a milk." Misty remains firm, "No, you can't have it."

For Misty, it did not matter whether Wynn had milk or coke or any drink; what mattered was Wynn's returning of the milk. She was less interested in excuses and more concerned about maintaining the same routine regarding "seconds" procedures and norms.

Essentially, Misty was creating order by enforcing and maintaining standards. In this case Misty gave an order and she was unwilling to negotiate with the resident. In general, an "orderer" expects her commands to be obeyed, becoming frustrated and anxious at any sign of resistance. The stratification of positions, between "orderer" and "orderee", often frames the interaction, thus anticipating certain outcomes. When "orderers" do not receive their desired response, a serious conflict could emerge, though now, there are two issues of concern, e.g., violation of the seconds procedure and failure to comply. In short, obeying orders reduces the possibility of further escalation.

Overlooking the infraction is also observed in this incident. Here, I observed the infraction but "had no intention of confronting Wynn." Our dissimilar reaction is a clear case of distinct interpretations, control perspectives and styles of staff. I overlooked his "milk attempt" because it did not seem significant to me. Misty, however, reacted immediately, possibly because the kitchen is her domain. She even compared resident dorm behavior to kitchen behavior, exclaiming that residents "get away" with numerous violations in dorms, but refused to allow such leniency in her territory.

The problem, in this case, is not so much with the resident but with staff. That is, staff are inconsistent when enforcing what they perceive as a rule violation, e.g., obtaining a milk during "seconds." After Wynn left, Misty angrily suggested that dorm staff are not as consistent as herself. She claimed, "these kids cannot accept NO for an answer. They are so used to getting away with things in their dorms that they think they're gonna get away with it here (kitchen). Well, NO! they're not going too!!" Thus, while staff overlook trivial violations, they may also refuse to respond to trivial violations because of differences in control styles, perspectives and territorial space.

A central issue related to "ordering" is: what do staff accept as sufficient compliance with an order? This concern is observed in a hip hop fashion called "sagging," which involves residents wearing their pants near the middle or below the buttocks. More often than not, long t-shirts are worn to cover underwear, and a belt strapped through the trouser loops to prevent pants from falling. The t-shirt is usually tucked in, though at times, t-shirts are worn outside the sagged pants to conceal the apparent violation. It is a style forbidden primarily because of its gang overtones, and according to the intake worker (Inga), "it looks bad." Many residents seem to enjoy this style, for it is part of their adolescent culture and appears unconcerned about a staff response.

"Sagging" does not directly challenge staff, and is not intended to arouse staff's attention. The covertness of "sagging' is witnessed in the casualness that accompanies the style. Residents who sag seem to do so more out of habit and faddishness than defiance; and when residents display this style, their demeanor seems calm and unworried. Staff are inconsistent when responding to "sagging." That is, sagging may go unattended, depending on the staff and particular residents.

For example, I observed an instance of sagging when residents of X-dorm entered the kitchen. As the single file line walked towards the food line, I noticed Scott (White male, last resident in line) wearing a pair of extremely sagged short pants (white pants). His shorts were so low that I could see his white boxer underwear, and the short pants that would usually stop at his thighs--were below his knees:

> As Scott passed me, we eyed one another and I asked him to "pull 'em up." Scott pulled his pants up over his buttocks, still they were somewhat low but I was satisfied with his compliance so I let it go...

There's a sort of leniency on the author's part, for Scott was obedient and I felt comfortable with the level at which he raised his pants. However, had Scott refused to make any adjustments on his pants, I would have had one of two options: I could have quietly accepted the refusal but documented Scott's sagging, notifying his counselor, so that this incident might be dealt with in a more formal, dorm and group setting. Or, I could have confronted the incident head on, insisting that Scott adjust his pants.

Consider the remaining portion of the incident:

> ...Then Tony (Black-male, short-stocky-build, new counselor in X-dorm) heard my request of Scott and immediately shot over like an angry air force lieutenant. Tony inspected Scott, demanding: "You're dressed inappropriately!!? Pull 'em up!!" Scott yells back: "I pulled them up!!" Tony: "Pull 'em up or get out of the kitchen!!" Scott angrily snatches his pants up; after which, he snaps at Tony, shrieking: "You happy now!!?" Tony: "Yeah, real happy!!"

Being a new staff member, Tony apparently had a need to take charge and establish himself as a strong counselor, putting up with little or no non-sense, and strictly enforcing institutional rules. There were definite limitations for Scott and Tony. For instance, had Scott refused, a loud argument was probable, in addition to Scott being penalized (possible lost of home pass or involuntary removal from OBH). In order to avoid any punishment and/or worsening his situation, Scott angrily complied, expressing his hostility by "snatching his pants up," and shrieking, "You happy now!!?" Tony received the most pleasure by not only receiving compliance, but further having the last words, e.g., "Yeah, real happy!!"

In part, Scott was not only reacting to Tony's hostile approach, but to the inconsistent standards of the institution. Tony and I delivered two distinct messages. Scott cites our inconsistency and lashes out by yelling, "I pulled them up!!" In addition to urging consistency among institutional representatives, Scott was inherently complaining that, "I've already pulled 'em up, why must 'I pull 'em up' again!!"

Tony was also constrained in this situation. Unlike an air force lieutenant, Tony could not physically remove Scott had he refused (state licensing and child abuse laws prohibit such behavior). But, by demanding that Scott "pull 'em up or get out of the kitchen," Tony was issuing an ultimatum. Scott declines any further challenge, conforming to proper standards; for it seemed clear to Scott (and myself) that Tony was accepting and responsive to any "Scott challenge." Here, neither staff seems concerned about the double standard. This indicates staff power irrespective of resident's feelings; we were not willing to view ourselves from the resident perspective, but our actions imply that residents must understand and conform to the staff world. Consequently, one may often hear residents complain "why (are) you doggin' me?" Or "why (are) you sweatin' me?" Our main concern then was resident compliance, and therefore maintaining staff authority and control.

There are times when staff give orders to a collectivity (a group of residents); the collectivity is dependent on one another for compliance. The lack of compliance could mean no further action or no further service, until compliance is meant. For instance, a "minimal noise level" is required during kitchen meals. As residents enter the kitchen, file through the food line, dine and eventually return for "second," residents may hold quiet conversations. Individual outbursts are typically sanctioned by staff and a group of noisy residents are confronted instantly. Such was the case when W-dorm residents filed through the food line:

> W-dorm residents were first to go through the food line, and entered rather loud in that they were noisy and banging their silverware on the metal counter. Two kitchen crew residents, working in the serving area (washing dishes), contributed to the noise by agitating W-dorm residents. Shawn (kitchen cook, serving the dinner meal) confronted both parties, shouting, "Quiet down!! Its too loud in here!!!" Shawn repeated himself for not everyone heard him and the noise level remained high. Though this time, his demand was louder, "QUIET DOWN!!!" He then faced the area of kitchen crew workers, and further demanded that they too "quiet down!" The residents became silent with their attention drawn to Shawn. As he reached for his first plate, Shawn seemed more comfortable about serving residents.

Cooks have authority to refuse service until residents are sufficiently quiet. Residents understand this, and further recognize that they may be asked to leave the kitchen if cooks remain dissatisfied with residential noise level. At second issuance of the order, the collectivity became "silent" primarily because of the sanctions available to the cook and their desire to eat first. Had Shawn applied sanctions, W-dorm residents may have returned to their dorm and eaten last. Alternatively, kitchen crew workers could have faced firing or suspension had they remained noisy. But the entire collectivity responded to Shawn's order, e.g., "quiet down," keeping in mind that one W-dorm resident could have effected the outcome of the group.

In the final analysis, while residents appear disturbed by orders, they seem to have few options when orders are given. The social and institutional factors contribute to staff's willingness to give orders and residents' limited choice options. Again, the bottom line for staff is not the emotional state of residents, but obedience to orders.

Hands-On Correction

Hands-on correction involves staff physically "snatching" or "grabbing" (e.g., reacting) an item from a resident that is situationally prohibited. It is the item itself that lead staff to react impulsively, leaving little or no room for negotiation. Hands on correction is examined in the context of an actual "snatch" and "grab", revealing again, the spontaneous situational response available to staff. What situations, then, cause staff to react impulsively? And, to what extent might staff have used another control style?

Correcting violations instantly, without the possibility of negotiation or resistance, appears to be the idea behind snatching. It clearly reduces physical struggle and in some cases, the period of verbal confrontation. "Snatching" a popsicle from a resident was the method used by staff to correct a resident's wrongdoing. Here, the resident proceeds through the food line to obtain a dessert yet fails to acquire the necessary food which entitles him to that dessert. Consider their encounter:

During dinner, I noticed Powell who appeared hostile, walk straight through the food-line, bypassing the food counter and other X-dorm residents in front of him, going straight to the dessert (ice cream popsicles). Residents are not suppose to eat dessert unless they eat a salad or a full meal. Powell had neither, and I watched him as he proceeded past the other X-dorm residents, and food counter—straight to the dessert. Powell picked up a dessert and left the food area. Don (X-dorm counselor) was standing at the end of the food counter (near the exit door of the food line), watching his residents. As I proceeded towards Powell, I informed Don of what Powell had done. Don then took over. Powell was about to sit down—when Don and I approached him. Don angrily said, "Where's your food!?" Before Powell could answer, Don insisted that "You're supposed to have dinner with your dessert!!" Powell explains, "I ate when my mother came." While reaching and snatching the popsicle out of Powell's hand, Don reminds,

"You cannot have this unless you eat dinner!" Don and I walk away towards the exit door of the food line. Don then unwraps the popsicle and eats it; while Powell returns to the food line for dinner, picking up another popsicle.

Residents are not permitted "dessert only" for dinner. In lieu of a balanced meal, residents are required to have a salad or a complete meal or both before obtaining a dessert. Don's response to the violation illustrates a type of harsh insensitivity by physically correcting the resident's behavior. Don actually snatched the popsicle from Powell (resident) to instantly correct what he (and the O.D.) viewed as an infraction.

Like Misty, Don was less interested in excuses and rationalizations but more interested in maintaining a rule, a rule that prohibits dessert without dinner. Upon being informed of the violation, Don was able to remedy the problem without much commotion or excitement. Though Powell explains his reactions, he too is aware of the rule, and Powell returns for food and dessert. Don is further acting on information supplied by a superior, e.g., the O.D. Don does not question the information but simply acts on it, suggesting obedience to authority, expecting residents to exhibit similar behavior. The O.D.'s detection of the violation and subsequent revelation to Don, indicates that the O.D. wants something done about the violation. The actions by Don and O.D. reveals that they are on the same side, situationally guarding against covert and underground activity of residents.

There are many ways that this infraction could have been handled, but Don chose hands-on correction. When someone snatches an item, one often reacts in ways that indicate anger, bewilderment and a longing for item return. Thus the nature of a snatch is to catch someone off guard, thus surprising the "snatchee." Snatching suggest that one (the "snatcher") not only anticipates resistance, but wishes to avoid as much conflict as possible, e.g., a "tug of popsicle."

As a method of control, snatching may accomplish immediately what negotiation would accomplish in minutes, hours or days. It implies a certain impatience on the part of the "snatcher" in that instrumentally, staff desire quick resolution, moving on to other control duties. Don's method also seems to emanate from his anger of not personally catching the violation, and feelings that Powell has somehow duped him, in the face of a superior.

Under what conditions are social control agents likely to yell, and then grab prohibited objects from minors? The following encounter is another example of "on-hands correction." This case examines a resident who smokes a cigarette in an unauthorized area. Shari (staff) was so stunned that she "yelled", then "grabbed" the cigarette out of his hand. While smoking is permitted, residents may only smoke in designated dorm areas. Donnell (Z-dorm resident) possessed a lit cigarette as he left the kitchen, and staff observing were shocked by his boldness. It was as if staff's reaction was habitual in that staff sought to immediately correct his actions. In short, "yelling and grabbing" became a reflexive method of correcting a rule violation. Consider the following excerpt:

> Shari (Z-dorm staff) and I were in the O.D. office talking when we both noticed Donnell walking out of (away from) the kitchen with a lit cigarette. We observed him as we looked outside the O.D. glass window. We were not looking for him, though as he passed we simply turned our heads in response to his motion.
>
> Seeing the cigarette shocked Shari and myself, hence our immediate reaction was to try to obtain his attention. I yelled out, "Yeah man!!" Shari, with her high pitched voice, screamed, "Donnell!!" After hearing our voices, Donnell attempted to hide the cigarette in the cup of his hand; he looked stunned, as if wondering, 'why are they yelling at me.' Donnell hid the cigarette but we saw him exhale smoke and could see smoke coming from the cup of his hand. In a demanding voice, I ordered, "Come here!" Donnell approached the O.D. window (which has a small opening), then Shari scolded him, "What are you doing with that cigarette!?" Before he could answer, Shari rushed out to confiscate the cigarette; literally grabbing it out of his hand. Donnell gave us an innocent look as if he was surprised by our actions. He said to Shari in the process of her taking the cigarette, "I didn't know." Neither Shari nor myself believed him, for why would he "cup" the cigarette if he were not aware.

Again, we witness a routine, almost spontaneous reaction by staff, who interprets the resident's behavior as deviant. Such reactions are in part habitual, spontaneous and sometimes unconscious. It is an indication that staff's reaction to certain rule violations may in fact be internalized. These responses can only be habitual and unconscious if such encounters are repetitious. The repetition emerges into a pattern, which could lead to reacting without thinking or acting spontaneously. But maintaining order through routine confrontations and correction is common at OBH. This gets at the stability of the institution, and the extent to which staff are capable of responding to emergencies and authority challenges by residents.

Parents often "yell and grab" at infants/toddlers who possess a dangerous object and about to place it in their mouth. They also "yell and grab" when toddlers are near fire or about to walk in the streets unattended. Frequently, "yells and grabs" are simultaneous, though at times they as separate, like in the case of Shari yelling at Donnell then grabbing the cigarette. Parents "yell and grab" to socialize, control and protect. Staff "yell and grab" to control, thus preventing the object (cigarette) from reaching his mouth. The ideal is to "grab it" before it is used or consumed. Then, a more rational explanation, by staff or parents, follows the grab, whether it involves cigarettes or dangerous objects.

Conversely, staff are less likely to snatch earrings, or for that matter, pull-up sagging pants of residents. Hands-on correction has certain limitations, and staff must learn what is appropriate to snatch, grab or pull-up. Hands-on correction is designed to handle minor violations quickly, without much resistance or repercussion. Pulling-up sagging pants could have messy implications. Residents may charge staff with pulling pants down or molestation. Similarly, grabbing a lodged earring is not as smooth or swift as snatching a popsicle. It is quite probable that there would be some injury to the earlobe. Hands-on correction then requires a certain skill level, experience and common sense. That is, A-resident and B-resident may have two different reactions to a popsicle snatch by staff. Consequently, staff must know which strategy of correction to apply for specific residents.

Requesting

The final situational remedy involves "requesting." Simple requests consist of asking residents to stand back, go to bed and lower radios. Requesting was experienced when I accidentally noticed Sanchez (resident) wearing an earring backwards. Earrings are prohibited because they symbolize gang attire and affiliation. Dressing in certain gang affiliated colors (red and blue) is also prohibited, for gang colors produces anxiety among staff and gang members. Moreover, it is easier to work with and treat a collectivity when certain gang barriers are absent. But the fact remains, regardless of how much staff attempted to eliminate gang symbols, the gang was very much alive at OBH. That is, though residents cannot wear red or blue, various gang gestures were evident. For example, in speech patterns (slang), hairstyles (duck tale), certain strolls (walks), poses and underground communication. Clearly, these situations are much more difficult to detect and confront objectively. But this gang attitude and sentiment seems enmeshed in the mystic of gang members and certain non-gang members, alike. Staff do not always sanction gang attire, particularly "Crip" blue and "Blood" red. Consequently, these inconsistencies send perplexing messages, which may lead to minor infractions, placing staff and residents in a type of "negotiated bargaining" position.

After discovering his earring, I felt compelled to privately confront and suggest to Sanchez (resident) that he remove the earring from his ear. "Requesting" became the method by which I controlled this encounter, as an institutional representative. The observation occurred as follows:

> As Z-dorm residents were walking through the food line, Sanchez said hi to me, extending his hand to shake mine. I was sitting next to the door entrance to the food line, though as he turned away, I noticed an earring in his ear. (NOTE: Had he not spoke and shook my hand, I may have never noticed his earring). The earring was placed in his ear backwards, thus it appeared he was trying to hide it...

In this case, the staff recognized a rule violation and confronted the resident. Recall that Sanchez initiated the greeting by saying "hi" and "extending his hand to shake mine." All residents do not routinely speak to or greet staff; in fact, Sanchez was the only resident to jar my attention by acknowledging me. Our friendly relationship may have inspired this acknowledgement. His greeting also expresses a kind of humanness that is experienced within the institution and a general respect for authority. This accounts for my specific method of confrontation; that is, "I asked him to step out of the food line so that we might sit and talk." Sanchez complied, allowing me to address him apart from his peers.

Consider the reminder of the incident:

> ...I asked him to step out of the food line so that we might sit and talk. He was somewhat hesitant; yet when he sat, I asked him, "what's that in your ear?" He said, "an earring." Author: "does your staff know that you have an earring in your ear?" Sanchez remarked, "Yeah." Author: "Well, why don't you take it out; that way we won't have any problems." He then stalled, saying that the earring was in his ear to keep the hole open. I commented, "that's o.k. you probably look better without the earring in your ear anyway." Sanchez took the earring out of his ear and angrily returned to the food line.

Given our relationship and initial handshake, I felt comfortable asking Sanchez to "step out of line," thus lessening the possibility of embarrassing him and avoiding a scene. We displayed a mutual respect, because upon recognizing the earring, I could have confronted Sanchez on the spot, causing a scene that would required more energy. But I chose a very calm and non-threatening approach.

Sanchez's hesitancy suggested that he should be cautious within our encounter, because it was unusual for ODs to arbitrarily pull residents out of line. When I requested that Sanchez "step out of line," he not only complied but appeared puzzled as to the nature of my inquiry. Moreover, had Sanchez done no wrong, why should he not comply? I assumed that we were operating under a similar value system, e.g., innocent until proven guilty, and complying (sitting) implied a certain amount of innocence.

Notice, however that after Sanchez was seated, I came straight to the point, "I asked him, 'what's that in your ear?' He said, 'an earring.'" Alternatively, Sanchez could have acted oblivious to my question, but he was very honest, yet clever in his forthcoming response: "Author: 'does your staff know that you have an earring in your ear?' Sanchez remarked, 'Yeah.'" Since his staff was in a different kitchen location, Sanchez cleverly answered in the affirmative, for I could not immediately verify his reply, and had I not accepted his response, I would have exerted much energy locating his staff and confirming or contradicting his story. But chances are that Sanchez would have changed his story in the presence of his staff.

Actually, my question (does your staff know that you have an earring in your ear?) poses a specific problem for Sanchez. The underlying implication is really: Your staff does not know of your earring, and if she did, you would not be wearing it. Sanchez then finds himself in a situation where he must say "Yeah," otherwise it lessens his chances of defeating authority and keeping his earring lodged. In a sense, Sanchez had little other choice; still I bypassed his answer because of my knowledge of the rule. Note that Sanchez's "yeah" response may be a result of his staff seeing the earring, though ignoring it. Nevertheless, Sanchez and I were conscious of the possible sanctions that could occur; and, there was no need to complicate the issue by inquiring whether his counselor approved the earring; for obscuring the earring was not necessary had his counselor granted permission.

Staff's response and encounter with Sanchez is a good example of a spontaneous control method, requesting. Our negotiation, through talk, was not egalitarian though Sanchez was clearly attempting to keep the earring lodge. He realized that "the staff excuse" was not working and he unsuccessfully returned to a humanistic approach, seeking an appeal to my sense of humanity and compassion, e.g., "the earring was in his ear to keep his hole open." Presumably, he sought to redefine the situation, but my knowledge of the rule broke off further discussion. It follows that staff's interpretation and response to trivial, minor infractions—frames the role of staff, the definition of the situation, the position of the resident and the realness of the rule. For the structure of the encounter is framed by the prohibition and the method used to correct the violation.

Requests are often made by staff to residents so to maintain some measure of control. For instance, when staff issue evening snacks that are popular among residents, e.g. cookies or candy bars, staff often encourage residents to "stand back". In such cases, residents rush staff (and the snack box) in an effort to obtain their snack first. Staff's typical response is, "I need you guys to stand back; give me some space. There's enough snacks for everybody." Here staff are concerned about residents receiving more than one snack, thus not having enough for all dorm residents. Bed requests are common particularly among residents who linger in the restroom or sit at their desk writing letters, after bedtime hours. During her final walk though the dorm, Mary Ann was surprised to find Evans (resident) writing at his desk. She asked him to "go to bed," and used further leverage by informing him that "the night man is here and will write you up if you're not in bed when he checks this room." Finally, lowering radios are regular requests. That is, at bedtime William seemed bothered by Garcia's (resident) oldies; thus William left X-dorm office, going straight to Garcia's nearby room, asking, "lower your radio, Garcia."

The significance of requests is that they are not designed to belittle residents; rather, their intent is to provide a positive atmosphere on which residents may respond. They are intended to leave residents with a good feeling about themselves and the encounter. In the long run, staff requests of residents may lead to improved relationships (between them) and an increased willingness by residents to conform. While residents seem to respond more favorably to requests---orders, snatches, yells and grabs seem to have the opposite effect. That is, staff appear less concerned about the personal well-being of residents when such control techniques are used. Staff's primary concern is compliance. Nevertheless, situational responses have everything to do with the circumstances surrounding the violation.

In conclusion, while several other scenarios are available, the above cases represent the process by which staff interpret and respond to minor rule violations. It is a process that develops a life of its own, placing staff in positions to appraise and determine an appropriate action. Rarely are residents sanctioned for petty rule violations, like loss of home pass or early bed. But, trivial violations are handled rapidly and with relative ease, e.g., put the cigarette out, put the milk back, quiet down, pull your pants up, take the earring out, lower your radio. Encounters that receive situational control are generally not serious violations; in fact, these minor rule infractions give staff an opportunity to address, and remind residents of institutional rules and their obligation to comply with them. Resistance from residents is minimal, if at all, which again gets at the trivial nature of these violations. The real issue is correcting behavior that staff view as incorrect; how correction is achieved depends on the situation and staff.

The use of situational remedies by staff is routine and quite frequent, yet, such an issue is unexplored in the literature. It is fair to assume that the lack of "situational exploration" is due to its success, e.g., in most cases, situational remedies "work." Moreover, the problem is dealt with, and without an institutional record of it occurring. Escalation of situational remedies provides a higher probability of institutional documentation, requiring now, an institutional response.

There are times however when situational remedies do not obtain their desired results, e.g., when hands-on correction goes wrong. Billy (OBH recreation supervisor) was involved in a situation that "blew up" in his face. That is, Billy was refereeing a basketball game between OBH residents and Lee Boys' Home (LBH) residents. According to OBH players and OBH basketball coach (Kip), Billy made a "bad call" causing coach Kip to become very upset, throwing his cap on the gym floor and scolding the referee (Billy). A fight ensued between Wheaton (OBH player) and an opposing LBH player. Rather than simply separating the two combatants, Billy (referee) grabbed Wheaton away from the other player and "slammed" him on the hard concrete gym floor. This provoked many OBH residents (Williams, Haynes, Burd) to become extremely angry with Billy, charging in his direction. Haynes (Z-dorm resident) pointed his finger in Billy's face, threatening and swinging simultaneously. Haynes landed a punch near Billy's eyes, breaking his glasses. Soon, Kip intervened by placing himself between Billy and OBH residents, and physically forcing Billy into the weight room, securing and locking the door.

Here, hands-on correction resulted in a brawl primarily because "player separation" was handled improperly. This situation clearly got "out of hand." Again, it gets at the competency of staff in recognizing the limitations and possible messiness of this approach. Hands-on correction can work and has worked well for staff who understand its strengths and weaknesses. But staff must realize that grabbing or snatching happens "in a flash," leading to actions that one may later regret but cannot change. It is within these parameters (the immediacy of grabbing or snatching, hands-on correction) that perceptions of staff are established, and sometimes maintained.

Institutional Responses

The key distinctions regarding situational remedies and institutional responses concern formal-extended punishment, written documentation, and the likelihood of external staff becoming personally involved.

Unlike situational remedies, institutional responses to resident rule violations assume a more serious nature. Rule violations by residents are not uncommon, nor unanticipated by staff. For this reason there exist many rules, and forms on which to document infractions by residents. Consequently, staff perceptions of serious rule violations are often documented on incident reports, awol reports, dorm logs and/or the main log. Such documentation permits other staff to possess a formal, institutionalized knowledge of certain residential infractions. This is not the case with situational remedies; where violations are handled verbally, gesturally and immediately. Staff may "hear about" a resident "taking an extra milk," but such talk cannot be empirically verified with a document and sanctions are not likely.

Another important quality of institutional responses is that other staff (staff outside the problem dorm) learn about and may become involved in the problems. At the very least, documentation ensures that other staff can read about the incident. They may become involved when requested by other staff. Finally, institutional responses may involve punishment; there is a high probability of sanctions resulting from institutional violations; indeed, institutional responses are often selected in order to subject residents to formal, longer-term punishment.

Resident violations, which are documented, are not necessarily oriented towards staff. They may be directed toward another resident by fighting or arguing. Sneaking a girl in one's room during a co-ed (dance), vandalizing ones' room or breaking an office window could also spark incident reports by staff. Here it is important to recognize that writing an incident report is one method available to staff for responding to such violations. Incident reports and awol reports[2] are kept in the O.D. office for all staff to review. Copies are then made and distributed to administrators, dorm social workers, probation officers, and filed in the resident's on-site file. Consequently, incident reports are used by the aforementioned groups when reviewing the progress of residents and/or confronting the resident concerning reported incident.

Types of Punishments: "Consequences"

There is a wide range of sanctions that staff use to control and punish residents. The usage and administration of sanctions is typically subjective in that there are no set criteria (or manual) for issuing sanctions to residents for specific violations. For example, there is no specific sanction for stealing, disrespecting staff, failing to follow staff instructions, fighting, etc. This then places staff in a discretionary position to interpret the nature of violations and creatively administer punishments to deal with the problem.

Staff chose from a variety of sanctions that they view appropriate, and "consequential" (punishment) for a resident's violation. The punishments used by staff are divided into three categories, e.g., basic, significant, and collective sanctions. Such grouping signifies staff's interpretation of punishment severity. Basic punishment, then consist of sanctions that are not stressful or anxiety ridden for residents. Such punishments are not lengthy but "easy" to serve. Staff view basic punishments as "a slap on the hand," yet appropriate for their act (norm infraction). For example, writing compositions and room restriction (resident is not permitted to enter another resident's room without staff permission) are considered basic. Richard Martin (resident) "was placed on room restriction" because his "gang talk" and "verbal intimidation" could lead to fights. Denny (staff) writes: "He (Martin) was placed on room restriction as a means of keeping him from starting fights with other residents. He draws attention from other residents by his gang talk, disrespect and verbal intimidation." Similarly, Mike Kline's (resident) basic punishment consisted of writing a "250 word paper" because he engaged in "unauthorized conversations with persons across the alley, in back of V and W dorms." Other basic punishments include early beds, room time (resident must remain in room alone while other residents have free time), pool restriction, no smoking privileges, gym restriction, recreation room restriction (resident is prohibited from entering gym or recreation room), and juvenile hall threats.

Staff invoke basic punishments as a way to prevent more severe troubles for residents; they are like warnings. The fact that staff detect and sanction such infractions is almost a blessing in disguise. Gang talk, which could lead to fights, and talking to persons across the alley, which could lead to an influx of contraband, would in fact take punishment to the next level (were these situations to occur).

Thus, significant punishments take us to that next level in that staff wish to make an impact on residents. Its function is general deterrence, designed to jolt not simply the sanctioned resident but any and all other residents. That is, X-resident serves as an example of what could happen to others given similar violations. Unlike basic punishments, significant punishments are designed to produce resident anxiety. For example, loss of home pass often disturbs residents; similarly, placing residents "on hold" tends to arouse their anxiety in that residents are in limbo until the staff counsels them and decides on a final course of action. Generally, this means that the resident is unable to engage in off campus activities, e.g., field trips, home passes or other activities that are considered privileges, until his condition is clarified. The issuing of "no privs" or no privileges indicates that staff have reached a specific punishment. Resident who receive "no privs" cannot engage in program activities that are considered privileges, e.g., watching T.V. and videos, field trips, smoking, working in kitchen, home pass, recreational activities, etc. The resident may only participate in that which is required by the OBH program.

Mixon (resident) was placed "on hold" because he spat on Robb (staff). According to Robb, "Mixon was at Z-dorm, when he was supposed to be at the gym. I sent him back to V-dorm (his original dorm), Mixon then became very aggravated. He came down to the OD's office and then spit on me." Though Robb did not spit back or physically harm Mixon, spitting is the type of violation that could become personal, and thereby escalate their encounter. Seemingly, a significant punishment was not only inescapable, but necessary as an attention-getter for other residents.

Other significant punishments include juvenile hall contracts and status drops. Juvenile hall contracts are considered significant because contracts give residents two weeks to improve behavior or terminated to juvenile hall.[3] Status drops are significant because they represent downward mobility and limited autonomy. That is, statuses carry with them privilege, prestige, perception, responsibility and autonomy (independence). The higher ones' status the more privileges, prestige, responsibility and autonomy. There is an overall positive perception of high status residents. Lower status residents receive limited privileges, prestige, responsibility and autonomy. Residents are encouraged to earn higher statuses so that they might have more privileges, independence and eventually graduate. Thus when one receives a status drop, he not only limits his activity and perceptions once held, but he now must regain his status by conforming to the rules of the OBH program. After two weeks (status evaluations are held every two weeks), the resident is evaluated by other residents and staff to determine whether he is worthy of a status increase or decrease.

The final category concerns collective sanctions that effect an entire dorm and/or the entire Home. Under what conditions are collective sanctions administered? Closing the dorm or dorm closure indicates that an entire dorm has no privileges and cannot participate in off grounds activities. This sanction is issued when staff believe residents have information but are withholding it. For example, when the panic button is pulled (by a resident) yet no one admits or has knowledge of the violation, a dorm might be closed. Here, a lengthy group may commence to obtain information, but if residents refuse to "fess-up" the dorm could remain closed for an extended period. Obtaining information seems linked to home passes or some activity that residents desire to partake, e.g. camping or Disneyland trip. Thus, as an event approaches, more information surfaces or even a confession is made to permit the dorm to re-opened and return to its normal state.

Alternatively, an attack or violation on the generic structure of the Home may cause Home closure. For example, gang writing on (or in) Home vehicles, graffiti in the Home lobby, theft from the kitchen, defacing the Home bulletin board, breaking-in the laundry room may all contribute to Home closure. Here, the entire home is closed and residents are not permitted off grounds. Privileges like smoking, T.V., videos, recreation room and gym activities remain in tact. The violation is usually discovered by staff and initially reported verbally, then documented in an incident report. The verbal revelation and incident report is often addressed to "administration". The generic nature of the violation usually inflames administrators prompting them to inform all staff, and instruct staff to "process" the issue during group. If information does not spring forth regarding those who are involved, administrators may well close the Home, even before dorms (or dorm staff) are aware of problems and having proper time to process the problem.

For example, Henry Nash (executive director) closed the Home when he discovered profanity written on an enclosed bulletin board in the OBH lobby. This bulletin board is exclusively for OBH club members. The board list OBH clubs and OBH club members who have made specific financial contributions (to OBH). Small block letters are used to make changes, update contributions, add new club members, and new OBH clubs to the bulletin board. The bulletin board then is of interest to club members for updates and announcements.

Apparently, the bulletin board was left open and someone rearranged certain letters to read: "fuck opportunity home." Mina (Mr. Nash's secretary) and Octavia (morning O.D.) discovered the bulletin board changes, and informed the Executive Director (Mr. Nash) when he arrived. As word spread, many staff came to view and chuckle at the bulletin board defacement. Such defacement was not comical to Nash, who was quite disturbed. He immediately closed the Home, wanting to know how and who got into the locked bulletin board. He also referenced the disappointment OBH club members would express were they to read the comment. He personally informed all dorms of the home closure, instructing them to find out the responsible party or parties.

The next day Gonzales, X-dorm resident, confessed to Helena (X-dorm counselor), saying that he was 'just having a little fun.' The Home closure was lifted after an extensive conference with Gonzales, Helena and Nash. Generic infractions then are defined as significant (by administrators) and subject to collective sanction. This is one method of expressing administrative anger, disappointment and authority as well as conveying the unacceptability of such acts.

While the above punishments are generally used to control residents, staff most frequently rely on "no privs." Shari (Z-dorm counselor) noted that "no privs means you don't have nothin', nothin' comin'. You have nothin'." "No privs" then covers a whole range of activities that are considered privileges. Moreover, the length to which a resident is subject to no privs is left to the discretionary nature of staff. That is, a resident may receive "no privs" for one day, three days, one week, two weeks, etc. It depends on staff's perception of the violation. For example, according to Kara (Z-dorm counselor), Logan (resident) "was given 3 days" for an "OGA" (on grounds awol). Duran (resident) was sentenced to "one week's loss of privileges for alcohol involvement". Thomas (resident) was sanctioned "1 week no privs for vandalism" and social worker Rob Bans sentenced Loften and Mitchell to "2 weeks loss of privileges" because they admitted stealing "candy from the kitchen."

Again, staff's interpretation and definition of the situation determines the type and severity of punishment. Staff have been known to issue both multiple and singular punishments for resident violations. Though how is this achieved? That is, how do staff decide to invoke singular or multiple punishments? Like judges, OBH staff sentence residents based on the magnitude and/or quantity of offenses. The application of social control varies from case to case. Thus, residents who horseplay are likely to received singular punishments and those who fight may well acquire multiple punishments. The issuing of sanctions has everything to do with staff's perceived magnitude of the violation. Additionally, the quantity of offenses, however minor, may effect one's punishment. Quantity of offenses also gets at socio-historical factors regarding sanction application. That is, while at Opportunity Boys' Home, some residents develop a history of disrespecting staff or smoking in prohibited areas. Consequently, such history may be considered when applying punishments.

Regarding singular punishments, W-dorm residents Batiste, Neal, Marlo, Wheeler and Osuna received a four day pool restriction for "horse playing" in the pool. Terry (resident) was given "dorm work" for being suspended from school. According to Don Benton (counselor), Hilliard, Micheaux and Macias lost their "smoking privs" because "they admitted to smoking cigarettes...in the back of Z-dorm;" and finally, Oscar Gasp (Z-dorm counselor) sentenced Delamastra (resident) to an early bed because "minor was caught several times...boxing and wrestling on his bed with Kelly" (resident). Seemingly, staff viewed these infractions as minor thereby applying singular sanctions. The function of issuing sanctions is not only to maintain a certain normative structure, but to inform residents that they have gone too far. Overlooking infractions could lead to increased deviance.

Though singular, the magnitude of a violation could cause staff to apply the most severe singular punishment, termination. For instance, over time, one of the most important rules to develop was the "no touch rule" for fear of fighting between residents (e.g., "touch" in the sense of physical horseplay, sparring or assault). This type of "touching" was labeled "physical contact" (or "physical") and when it occurred, sanctioning was inconsistent. Periodically, however, one may hear a resident shout at another, "don't touch me!" or "get your hands off me!" The rule also applies in the direction of residents touching staff (and vice versa). In such cases, whether a penalty is administered is not in question, but rather, the type of sanction. Child abuse laws prohibited staff from "touching" residents, not to mention that touching residents is a questionable treatment practice. Only in cases of restraint are staff permitted to touch residents. This is not to say that staff do not "touch" residents. On the contrary, both groups "touch" the other (embrace, hug, handshake and even fight). The real question is: under what conditions do staff (or residents) hold the other responsible for an irritating "touch" or assault? When has the other gone too far?

According to Dora, "Jefferson (resident) became angry because he was penalized by me." He reacted by verbalizing his disgust ("you get on my nerves"), pulling her hair and grabbing her arm. Dora felt her authority had been grossly violated and rushed to Inga's (administrator) office to inform her, insisting on termination for Jefferson. Her request for termination suggest the severest penalty, indicating that she wanted to guard her safety against the possibility of additional attacks, and at least partial restoration of her authority.

Unlike singular punishments, multiple punishment involves applying more than one sanction to a rule violation or several violations. One could receive a punishment for each violation or simply acquire multiple sanctions for one violation. Staff possess huge discretion in this regard. The use of staff discretion depends on the situation and the type of relationships established between staff and resident. The following examples provide staff rationale for administering multiple sanctions.

Claude (Y-dorm counselor) issued multiple sanctions to Martin (Y-dorm resident) because of his dining hall fight with Hodge, W-dorm resident. According to Claude, "staff in the dining room stopped the physical contact (fight) and pulled both residents apart." Claude seemed noticeably upset and later placed Martin on hold, in addition to dropping his status and sentencing him to "7 days N/P" (seven days no privileges). Counselor, Jim issued a "drop of status and one week no privs" to Mitchell (resident) for failure to follow instructions. Apparently, Mitchell inquired whether he could accompany Jim and others residents as they walked to the store. Jim denied his request, but Mitchell nonetheless trailed the group. And finally, Dio (W-dorm counselor) was unwilling to give Neal (resident) his mail because of Neal's refusal to do his dorm job. According to Dio, Neal "began having a temper outburst, yelling and disrespecting staff in a threatening manner." Consequently, "Neal received 1 wk N.P. (one week no-privileges) for disrespecting staff, and placed on hold for his temper outburst."

Seemingly, staff issue multiple sanctions based on the perceived seriousness of the resident's infraction and/or staff's frustration with the experience. Moreover, multiple sanctions are designed to impact residents so to prevent or minimize subsequent violations. In either case, staff have authority to issue singular or multiple punishments, and while the severity of sanctions is left up to staff, residents are often unhappy with punishments.

Recording Punishments: Logs and Incidents Reports

Some punishments do not generate incident reports, but are recorded in other ways, e.g., dorm log or main log. Residents receiving early beds for sneaking (down) to the gym are generally recorded in the dorm log. Residents taking more than one snack are also reported in the dorm log, indicating to other staff that X-resident should not receive a snack the following evening because he took an additional snack without permission. The nature of the violation then has much to do with how and where it is recorded. Documentation only in the dorm log, and not in incident report form, indicates that staff does not view the violation as serious, but an infraction that needs recording so that other dorm staff are aware. Dorm logs are generally read by dorm staff working in that dorm, including night staff. Such logs are used to communicate with staff, providing a continuous account of daily dorm atmosphere, e.g., line-ups, kitchen & school behavior, resident evaluations, things-to-do, resident concerns, group issues and resident punishment. Thus when off-duty staff return to work, they are to read the dorm log, beginning at the point of their departure. This brings them up to date on dorm issues during their absence. Residents however are not permitted to read any log (main log or dorm log) and administrators rarely read dorm logs.

Punishments that are documented in the main log are usually documented elsewhere, e.g., incident reports or awol reports. Social workers and counselors typically wish to cover all bases in so far as a resident not being able to attend an outing or go on home pass. That is, they wish to inform all interested parties when residents lose certain privileges. This prevents residents from sneaking through the cracks, in that residents are required to check-out with the O.D.[4] before going home, and counselors are required to sign-out all residents before leaving grounds.

Thus, one of the principal persons to read the main log is the O.D. *All* staff may read this log, and some read it regularly, but the O.D. must be aware of all main log entries, e.g., for information and decision making purposes. Moreover, administrators review this log so they might receive a general feel for the functioning, activities and atmosphere of the Home. Main log entries however are made by *all* staff, and while certain punishments are recorded, other information is also included, e.g., awols, terminations, home visits, licensing visits, dorm closures, etc.

Incident reports then are official documents that are used by staff to report substance abuse, physical violence (fights), stealing, suicide attempts, school incidents, police involvement, alleged child abuse, night problems, illness or injury, sexually related incident, vandalism and other incidents that staff view as significant enough to officially document in this form. Incident reports typically involve problems among residents or problems with specific residents. The incident report form requires that staff describe incident, date incident, list those residents involved, list staff present during incident, and describe action taken by staff. As previously mentioned, incidents reports are official documents that are distributed among administrators, probation officers and placed in the resident's file.

When and how do staff decide to officially report rule infractions? There are varying reasons as to how staff decide to write incident reports; often situational conditions, personal reasons, what others might think and institutional appropriateness influences incident report writing. As mentioned, fights among residents, vandalizing Home property, theft among residents, sex play and suicide contemplation are all required documentation. Administrators are likely to question staff if such reports are missing, e.g., "where's the incident report?!" Yet when staff are disrespected (cursed, yelled at) by residents or a resident refuses to follow instructions, staff may well handle these situations by writing an incident report. Ricardo recounted one incident: "We were watching videos in the T.V. room, and Taylor (resident) kept makin' these burpin' noises. We couldn't hear everything so I told him to be quiet! The guys were telling him to 'shut up fool.' He kept agitatin' us with these noises. So I told him: You make one more noise and I'll write you up. He wouldn't stop, so I wrote him up and gave him an early bed." Other staff revealed that "I (Lori, staff) wrote up everything that Brice (resident) did to show Janette (Clinical Director) that he was not suitable for this place." Lori believed Opportunity staff were not equipped to treat Brice's neurotic problems. At the dismay of W-Dorm staff, Janette however insisted that W-dorm staff work with Brice. Raymond, on the other hand expressed, "covering my ass" was the main factor in writing incident reports, that is, he wanted to avoid any accusation of failure to report incidents that administrators would hear about "through the grapevine". And finally Evia conveyed that "Don (Z-dorm staff) told me to write it up." In short, Evia was new and unclear on what to do when an angry resident "trashed the dorm." Don, a more senior staff, told her to "write it up," e.g., write up the incident in incident report form.

Documentation then is done by staff and its function is to specifically record and describe behaviors of those involved. Below are examples of how staff describe and convey incidents in their reports, e.g., "running his own program" and "suicide" respectively:

> "Adrian walking around dorm displaying a T-shirt around his head with gang letters on front of it. He was placed on bed-rest[5] but never stayed in his room. He wasn't getting along with other residents of the dorm. He was very abusive and argumentative about everything that was confronted to him about his behavior. He did not follow staff instructions at all. He was also talking out of his bedroom window to W-dorm residents, when asked to stop. Again, he was abusive and wanted to argue every point and issue. He ended up running his own program." On the same report, Kevin wrote: "Social worker Marie Huson called later to check on dorm situation, and she was informed about Adrian's behavior."

> "Thomas reported to me that he attempted suicide by placing a ribbon around his neck and tying it to grill of air conditioning vent. He stated that the ribbon broke when he tried to put pressure on his neck." Raymond also writes that "M. Huson, on call supervisor, notified, O.D. notified resident to be red flagged, night staff to monitor resident."

The tone of incident reports as well as how and what staff convey is solely a staff decision. Staff convey anger, frustration and even concern depending on the situation; and in some cases, what they want done about certain violations. Moveover, certain incident reports, like suicide ideation, are also recorded in both dorm and O.D. logs as well as documented on night reports.[6] This is to permit everyone knowledge and caution regarding this volatile situation. By keeping room doors open, counseling the resident who contemplates suicide, and monitoring his room, staff make special efforts to control the situation. Unlike the suicide case, "running his own program" is an internal matter that does not deserve or receive the type of institutional attention given to suicide. Yet it was important to record given the resident's bed-rest infractions and the staff's inability to get him to follow the program. Such behavior often leads to specific punishments.

Summary

This chapter has examined "everyday control," e.g., how staff in a juvenile detention center experience and respond to everyday rule violations by residents. Staff reaction to resident infractions is largely based on staff perception. The crux of this process then involves staff's concern with maintaining order. Thus, the question of how order is maintained through doing control has been a major theme of this chapter.

Situational remedies and institutional remedies are two significant control responses available to staff. Situational remedies include staff efforts to control situations with resources personally available to them. This usually involves correcting a resident's infraction immediately and often without sanction. Situational remedies examined various control strategies, e.g., ordering, snatching, yelling and grabbing, and requesting. These control strategies get at the creative and spontaneous approaches used by staff to quickly resolve minor violations.

Institutional remedies are linked to more serious rule violations, which are handled through formal institutional procedures (incident reports, documentation in dorm and main logs, counseling-group sessions, etc) and agents outside the situation. Institutional responses require more investigative work and frequently result in formal punishment. The type of punishments used by staff are divided into three categories: basic, significant and collective. Moreover, staff's interpretation and definition of the situation determines not only the type, but severity of punishment. Hence staff have been known to issue multiple as well as singular punishments.

Finally, resident punishments are documented. Here, it is important to keep a formal record of residential behavior, in that record keeping assist staff in making key decisions about residents. For example, whether certain residents should receive a status increase or decrease; or whether certain residents are eligible for rewards; and whether resident progress (or lack thereof) should result in graduation or termination.

Notes

1. The kitchen department carries two types of milks, e.g., staff milk and resident milk. The only difference is the color of the cartons, that is, staff milk is orange, resident milk, red. Here, Misty was more concerned about Wynn picking up *any* milk.

2. An awol report is another type of document to be considered later.

3. See my discussion of "contracts" in the chapter on "resident leaving."

4. The main log is placed on the O.D. office desk.

5. Ordinarily, residents are placed on bed-rest by the OBH nurse, because they are diagnosed as sick. Residents who are on bed-rest are not to leave their rooms, except for restroom purpose and with staff permission. Food is delivered to the resident's room.

6. Night reports are written by day staff and received by night counselors, who work the over-night shift. Night counselors have access to incident reports, awol reports, dorm and main logs.

Chapter 5

Institutional Emergencies: Panic Button

Emergencies are inevitable throughout society; they occur on micro and macro levels, e.g., in homes, communities, schools, parks, hospitals, boys' homes, prisons and within countries. Most members of society are familiar with emergencies, and when they occur, members usually possess knowledge of what to do. Those who are not aware—quickly learn, labeling "X" occurrence an emergency and possibly acquiring a related response.

Emergencies are so universal and contemporary that rarely do we imagine emergencies having roots or origins. Given the nature of emergencies, there simply appears a response associated with solving problems. Then, following social crises, emergency evaluation (hindsight) occurs to improve individual and institutional responses. So, contemporary responses to emergencies are based on historical experiences as ways to improve social response.

Emergencies are associated with loud sounds and bright colors. Symbolically, sirens, bells, buzzers, certain human screams, flashing red and blue lights alert us to troubles that require special and urgent attention. When fire trucks are in route to fires or policemen pursue robbers, most members of society slow and move to the roadside. This behavior results in giving emergency vehicles priority during disasters. In fact, emergency vehicles are often accorded privileged parking and access. Those within emergency areas tend to *stand around* or slowly drive (looky-lous) to glimpse at the incident. Spectators are curious about what happened, whose involved, how emergencies are managed and possible heroic efforts. Without question, emergencies grab our attention and curiosity.

This society (USA) has partially prepared its members to respond to certain emergencies. Like in the case of natural disasters, e.g., hurricanes, floods, fires, and earthquakes specialists along with media make efforts to inform us (public) on what to do, how to do it, and severity of problem. Alternatively, society has developed an impersonal, institutionalized system of reporting emergencies, e.g., 911. When there are emergencies in the home (baby stops breathing) or school (school shooting), one may dial 911 to receive assistance. Consequently, a major feature of the sociology of emergencies is their *unpredictable quality*. If one could predict crisis, social response would not hold the same relevance. In fact, it ceases emergency status, becoming a calculated misfortune.

Emergencies additionally function to promote social unity, particularly with respect to natural disasters. When citizens are unexpectedly driven from their homes, unable to buy food, gas, clothing, electronically disconnected from society and uncertain about magnitude and longevity of disaster, a social solidarity among victims tends to emerge. The human quality of how to survive and/or how to control emergencies unfolds. That is to say, alternative forms of living develop as coping strategies to survive. Onlookers, near and far, sympathize with victims sending material donations (food, money, clothes, etc), writing encouraging letters, offering lodging and hosting celebrity benefits to raise funds and increase social awareness.

Emergencies clearly exist in our society, making them an integral part of one's life experience. Main actors can only anticipate their response not actual behavior during emergencies. Given that emergencies are unpredictable (we do not know when, where, or how they will occur), it is difficult to prepare by rehearsing one's response. Police and fire officials' train for emergencies, but typically, the general public does not. As a social fact then, emergencies clearly hold the quality of influencing our attitudes and behaviors in that we caution children to "look both ways before crossing," warning children of adult supervision while swimming, use of danger signs, fastening seatbelts and several other situational and institution precautions. In short, our previous stock of knowledge allows us to prevent emergencies before they happen; and efforts at preventing emergencies reduce social trudge within society.

Emergencies at OBH

An analysis of the panic button gets at how staff actually responds to institutional emergencies. In part, it is an examination of how staff restores crisis situations. Crisis situations suggest that severe troubles exist and that assistance is needed. No matter what the crisis, the ideal is to control such problems, returning OBH to some sense of normality. Unlike "everyday control," crises don't happen everyday, thus there are more or less established control strategies to restore order. This chapter addresses how control is done during emergency situations. It is interesting to explore the emergence of roles during emergencies, not to mention the innovative techniques in managing emergencies. For instance, one's formal status may have little to do with their acquired role during emergencies. Thus, the evolution of roles and overall control process during crises deserves attention.

At Opportunity Boys' Home (OBH), the sounding of the panic button signals an emergency; the panic button is associated with a loud buzzer, which alerts all staff (and residents) to a serious problem. Panic buttons are typically pulled (sounded) when there is a crisis or when dorm staff are unable to handle problematic situations, which includes fights between residents, possible riots, residents who are considered out of control, and residents who threaten staff. The panic button then, is used *anytime* there is a perceived emergency.

During in-service training, staff learn official procedures in responding to panic buttons. Staff are told where to locate the main panic button panel; where emergency buttons are within dorms; when to activate panic button; how to access the button and how general staff should respond to panic buttons.

Before installation of the panic button, there was virtually an ad hoc response to emergencies.[1] That is, a staff would tell a resident to "go get more staff!!" Or used the intercom to inform and command help, e.g., "All available staff report to X-Dorm," or use dorm-phones to communicate trouble and obtain assistance. This system was replaced by an up-to-date, state of the art emergency system. For instance, inside the five dorms, panic buttons were installed and mounted in very tactical locations, e.g., near the desk in dorm offices and in dorm hallways. These "spots" give staff rapid access to emergency buttons, whether inside or outside the dorm office, or dorm itself. The panic button is actually a 3x5 box mounted about waist high on the dorm walls. There is a hanging sting which staff pulls to activate alarms.

When the panic buttons has activated, a loud buzzer is heard throughout the Home. There are not separate buzzers for each dorm; there is a single buzzer. If the panic button panel (in the O.D. office) indicates W-dorm, it is assumed that an emergency existence in W-dorm; and presumably W-dorm staff are cognizant of the alarm sounding. But there is no alarm that activates in W-dorm and O.D. office, separately. The O.D. office contains the main emergency panel, which is designed to indicate emergency areas. Dorms do not have panels; they simply have panic buttons. The O.D. has both, panel and panic button.

The main panic button panel is located inside O.D. (Office of the Day) office, and mounted directly above entrance door. Opposite the door is a huge glass window permitting staff and residents to see inside, and the O.D. (or anyone inside the O.D. office) to see outside. The O.D. office is not meant to be a private place; part of its function is to receive, store and distribute information. One important source of information is found on the panel when the button has been activated. Each dorm letter and "O.D." office is inscribed on the panel; next to each inscription is a red light, which will flash when emergency buttons are activated.

The unprotected areas (areas without alarms) include gym, kitchen, school, chapel, social service office, business office, laundry room, recreation room and maintenance office. Of these, emergencies are most likely to occur in the gym, kitchen and school, for these are places residents tend to frequent.[2] Staff members in such locations phone O.D., informing him of the emergency and request activation of panic button. The O.D. remains in the office directing staff to the crisis location. Panic buttons may be activated from the O.D. office and any of the five dorms.

Hearing panic buttons throughout the Home, staff (social workers, line staff, recreation staff, & O.D.s) typically rush to the O.D. office looking through the window, at the panel, to determine crisis location. Some staff might call (the O.D.) inquiring about the crisis location while others see staff in route and in pursuit, asking and following them to the emergency area. In either case, staff members are required to initially locate the crisis, then rush to the scene. All staff however do not charge to the emergency scene. That is, responding to the panic button is largely dependent on staff availability. For example, if only one staff is covering (or working) "Dorm X", then he must remain in his dorm. Alternatively, two staff working

"Dorm X" would permit one staff to rush to the scene while the other covers the dorm. According to OBH policy, at least one staff member must supervise when residents are present; and residents are not permitted in dorms without staff.[3] Thus, OBH attempts to maintain two staff for every shift, in every dorm, but given the high turn over rate, this is an ideal condition. Procedurally, every available staff should respond to the panic button.

Recreation staff Robert inquired about why the panic button was referred to as the "panic button." He thought a better reference would be "emergency alarm." For Robert, other staff and even outsiders, labeling an emergency alarm as "panic button" has frantic connotations that could defeat the treatment purpose of OBH. Eventually, the institution hierarchy, recognizing that the behavior of staff (and sometimes residents) when responding to alarms was in fact panicky, chaotic and confused, questioned whether such a label, and therefore connotation was appropriate. In their October meeting, the clinical director as well as OBH social workers were debating and considering this same issue. Their concern with residential treatment and the term's frantic implications persuaded them to change the phrase from panic button to emergency button. Phil (Z-dorm social worker) explained that "we changed it because panic buttons sounds like everybody's in a panic...We felt that better suits the situation, even though people are probably panicking when they pull the button." Regardless of this formal change, staff references to the button as "panic button" remains.

Charging to the Scene

Staff response to alarms and crisis handling is clearly worth examination. This gets at staff's control abilities, their feelings on the panic button, how one should respond and whether practical response changes are necessary. Thus, two examples of emergencies are provided to illustrate practical responses to the panic button and the processes by which staff re-establishes order in the institution.

The "panic button" sounded around 7:30pm in V-dorm. When I arrived I observed Dio (W-dorm case aide) and Raymond (V-dorm counselor) struggling with Ford (V-dorm resident, Black-male, 14 years of age). They were trying to restrain him as he resisted by not letting them obtain a firm hold. Raymond tried to contain his upper body (chest area) while Dio attempted to hold Ford's arms. Suddenly, Don Benton (Z-dorm counselor, Black male) stormed into V-dorm office, and without question or thought, went directly for Ford's legs, attempting to obtain a solid hold so that he could lift him. Rob Bans (X-dorm social worker, Black male) followed Don and grabbed at Ford's other leg. Then, the four of them lifted Ford (who is still wiggling), carrying him out of the V-dorm office.

As the four staff removed Ford from the office, I momentarily observed Julie (White-female, V-dorm counselor) instructing a crowd of on-looking residents to "go back to your rooms!! Get out of the way!!" She appeared very uncomfortable; I noticed a blank, frightened facial expression. Though her voice was loud, because of the very nature of the situation, it was not very forceful, and residents did not move or respond quickly to her instructions.

I followed as the four staff carried Ford down the hall, up the stairs and out of V-dorm. Outside of the dorm (on the concrete area, near the kitchen), Ford was kicking and squirming, trying to pry himself lose from staff hold. The staff was stationary, not moving in any direction, just simply gripping, grabbing and adjusting their hold on Ford. There was no direction from anyone (staff), no one said anything. But while we were carrying Ford out of the office, I thought I heard someone (possibly Dio) say carry him to one of the rooms. But we ended up outside with no direction. Finally, I said: "Take him to the O.D.'s office."

Arriving in the O.D. office, we struggled with him further. The four staff struggled to forcefully seat Ford so that he might settle. While seating him, staff held him down as Ford was trying to loosen himself from staff hold. Then Ford shouted, "Let go of me!! Let go of me!!" Dio, one of the primary restrainers, replied, "We'll let go of you when you calm down!!" Now, there were three staff restraining Ford, e.g., Dio, Raymond, and Don. Rob stood behind the O.D. desk observing and I stood near the O.D. door observing; other staff, like William of X-dorm and Ricardo of Y-dorm hung around outside the office; Mandy was near the area but did very little. Soon Ford demanded again, "Why are you puttin' your hands on me?! Let me go!" Dio: "We'll let you go when you calm down."

Eventually, staff did loosen Ford but Ford remained hyper. The staff (Dio & Don) stood close around him while Raymond sat on the O.D. desk facing Ford. Staff hovered over Ford to prevent him from running out of the office. As Ford sat, he would direct his energetic anger towards Raymond, yelling, "Man you don't have no business grabbin' me. My arms are hurting, you know! You don't have no business grabbin' me!" Then Ford jumped up as if to swing on Raymond. Dio, Don and myself immediately restrained Ford, as Raymond jumped off the O.D. desk with his guard raised. Raymond's hands were raised, but his fists were not clenched—raised to block any possible blows or punches by Ford. Ford, on the other hand, had his fist clenched in a rage of anger, for he was about to attack Raymond. With his guard raised and slightly extended, Raymond shouted, "Don't do it!! Don't do it!!" I sensed that had Ford hit Raymond, Raymond would have returned with his own set of punches. Ford did not hit Raymond. Seeing that Raymond was the source of Ford's anger, Dio ordered: "Leave the room, Raymond. Leave the room!!" Author: "Yeah, get out of here!!"

Raymond left the office and stood outside in the hallway, where he could hear the entire conversation. We sat Ford back down and began to settle him. Dio did most of the talking. He began with whether Ford was hurt and indicated that if he were injured, we would get him medical attention. Dio then asked about Ford's family; that is, "When was the last time you seen your mother?" And whether he wanted to call her. Ford remarked that his mother was in New York and that the only reason he was in L.A. was because he was visiting an aunt but while visiting, Ford was arrested for a crime. Dio established that Ford's only family contact was his aunt, but further discovered that his aunt did not want him because of his behavior. Then Dio went further to draw an analogy between placement and Juvenile Hall. In effect, Dio said that when residents fight or cause problems in the hall, they are placed in a "box"[4] as a consequence of their poor behavior. "But in placement, there are no boxes. We don't have a place where we can lock you down when you're out of control. So if you can't control yourself here, you probably shouldn't be here."

Dio calmed Ford and would eventually leave the O.D. office while Rob Bans continued counsel. Seeing that Ford was calm Don eased out and so did I. I went to V-dorm to speak with Raymond concerning the origin of the incident. Now according to Raymond, Ford was in the restroom sitting on the window ledge, leaning back out of the window, as if he were going to fall out. Raymond instructed Ford to come inside so that he would not fall out. Raymond then mentioned that he visualized Ford falling out of the window, and heard the "ghost" (administration) he would face had Ford fell. Ford refused, saying—according to Raymond, 'no, I'm not gonna move inside.' Consequently, Raymond grabbed Ford, pulling him inside (off the ledge) and into the dorm office. While in the office, they began to struggle. That is, Raymond tried to restrain Ford while Ford fought Raymond off. Raymond then instructed Julie to pull the "panic button," which would trigger rapid staff assistance.

When the Ford situation was calmed and while Raymond and I, and others (staff) later sat in the nurse's office reviewing the event, Raymond repeated his version three separate times, for different key people would trickle in inquiring about the incident. (Marie Huson, V-dorm social worker, Raymond's supervisor; Mandy, Z-dorm social worker who also observed the Ford incident; and Rob Bans, X-dorm social worker, also assisted in restraining Ford).

The issue of course is restoring order or restoring control. How do staff restore a chaotic situation? Before order is restored, staff must *get there* (to the specific location of the emergency). Without staff *getting there* order is delayed, and the emergency could take on a profoundly new character. So rushing to the scene and *getting there* is significant regarding a "show of force" to control the situation.

As staff members respond, they are acting in concert. There is a type of consistency to every staff that arrives, that is, no staff questions why Ford is being restrained (or even why the panic button was pulled). Moreover, every staff (except Judy) and myself assist in restraining some portion of Ford's body. Consequently, when the panic button sounds, for staff, it is an indication that there is trouble and something must be done. Thus seeing Raymond struggling with Ford upon entry supplies first hand evidence of trouble, thereby a need to assist a fellow staff. In short, staff do not ask questions, because there questions are answered witnessing the struggle between Raymond and Ford; that is, somehow Raymond is in trouble and incoming staff are doing what they can to rescue him and restore order. Police operate in a similar fashion. When an officer is being beaten by a citizen fellow officers typically come to his aid without asking questions for they can see the problem.

There is also the sense of "we-ness" in that "we" (staff) must work together to quell the incident. Here then roles tend to emerge. As various staff arrive, they recognize that more restraint is needed so they become "restrainers". Julie, on the other hand, became a "traffic control counselor," in that she realized that staff needed space and residents were clogging up the much needed hallway, so she yelled, "go back to your rooms!! Get out of the way!!" She was directing hallway traffic. Raymond played the temporary "leader" for he was initially responsible for restraining Ford and instructing Julie to pull the panic button. But interestingly enough roles change as the setting change, e.g., Raymond became less and less of a "leader" and more and more of a "follower"/"restrainer." Eventually, Dio became the primary "leader" and "head counselor" in an effort to calm the situation and restore order.

Part of restoring order was to remove Ford from V-dorm, separating him from other residents in V-Dorm. At times, unruly residents may cause an entire dorm to become chaotic. The idea was to isolate Ford, so we could work through his problems. Staff, like police officers, prefer questioning residents privately rather than publicly in order to avoid a public evaluation and interference. Separation then simply permits better control of the emergency. This phenomenon of social separation is common among emergencies in general. That is, officials and citizens are separated by physical barriers and/or perceived barriers. Typically, it is the formal social control agent who defines and establishes boundaries between authorities and citizens.

Yet by isolating Ford, he channeled his anger towards Raymond, who in Ford's mind was the source of his "troubles." Raymond was then told to leave while Dio counseled and stabilized Ford. Essentially, staff will do whatever is necessary to obtain control, including removing staff who are perceived as threats to order, restraining residents, placing residents in alternative dorms, allowing residents to smoke to relieve pressure, and even counseling to secure the situation.

This next incident illustrates how staff intervention may escalate a confrontation between residents. While staff function as social control agents, at times, they are used by residents to gain institutional status among their peers. Consider the conflict between Haney and Duran, focusing on how Haney reaches over staff to fight Duran, signifying his public attempt to achieve prestige.

As I walked the hall of X-dorm, I noticed two residents, Haney and Duran, arguing in room seven. I stood in the hallway observing them but they were simply arguing; thus I watched just to see how far they would go. Haney yelled at Duran saying that he would kick his ass, but Duran simply walked away to the other side of the room. Haney followed Duran but he kept walking away. Really, it appeared as though Haney was blowing off steam in Duran's face. But Haney got louder and louder with each threat. Then Jim and Venessa (X-dorm counselors) came to room seven to investigate. Jim entered room seven and stood between Duran and Haney. Now, Haney became very disturbed, trying to reach over Joe to attack Duran. Duran questioned, "Why didn't you do that before?" (Suggesting, why did not Haney attack or come after Duran before staff arrived?). Haney became worse as he tried to fight through Jim. I took Duran and we walked down the hall into room two and closed the door. Venessa went to the staff office to sound the panic button. As Haney ran after us, I yelled to Jim, "hold him Jim!!" Jim was able to hold Haney off until we got in room two. I imagined Haney, who is bigger than Jim, broke loose soon after we were safely in the room. After closing the door, there was a bang but I did not open the door.

After the string of bangs ceased, I left room two closing and locking Duran in the room. I met Venessa outside the room where she hurriedly instructed, "Close the door!! Close the door!!" I closed the door and Haney was in the hallway being held back by Jim. He loosened himself from Jim, rushing room two. I intercepted Haney by grabbing and holding him around his waist. By then, Phil Simmons and Don Benton responded to the panic button; X-dorm residents had surrounded the hallway and day room area. Hence, as I held Haney, I walked him into the Day room, sat him down and began questioning him. Don, Phil and Jim also surrounded him, while the residents looked on from the public area of the day room.

I asked Haney, as he sat and we stood, "What's the problems?" Haney, "Nothin'!!" Author, "Nothin'?!! That's a lot of "nothin' for you to act that way!! What did he do? Did he push you, hit you, kick you!?" Haney shakes his head in a no motion, then says a calm, "no." Here Haney is well aware of his resident audience, thus he seems to have every intentions of "keeping face" in their presence. When I realized that my questioning was going nowhere, I suggested, "Let's go to the office!" Haney arose and went to the office without struggle. X-dorm office is next to room two, where Duran was secured. As I pulled out my keys to open the office, Haney again charged room two. This time, Don and Jim held Haney off, but it didn't take much, and it appeared, Haney was still performing for his audience of peers.

Entering the office, I ordered Haney to "take a seat!" Haney acted as though he was not interested in sitting, but he did and I sat near him on the arm of the couch. Jim (X-dorm counselor) was involved in the conference and he positioned himself away from us—behind the desk. Again I probed Haney's reasons for his behavior, inquiring, "Why are you doing this?" Haney, "'Cause he stepped on my foot" (Haney had socks on, no shoes). I responded in a tone that suggested that I could not believe that Haney could act-out for such a petty action. Author, "He stepped on your foot?" Haney had to make it more serious, commenting, "Yeah, he pushed open my door and stepped on my foot." Jim, sitting behind the desk, couldn't believe it either, threatening, "Do you want to lose your pass?" Then I interjected, "You know, you guys horseplay all the time and who knows when you're serious." Then I was reminded of "the Haney show" and turned to Jim, commenting, "Jim, he wasn't gonna do nothing, 'cause if he was, he would have done it before staff came!" This remark angered Haney immensely. His voice raised and was more challenging to me. Haney claimed, "No, I was gonna kick his ass!!" Author, "No you wasn't, 'cause if you was, you could have done it while he was there in the room. So why didn't you do it then!!!?" Haney, "Because he kept walkin' away!!" Author, "Yeah, he walked away but if you wanted to kick his ass, you could have!!" Then Haney became enraged, directing his anger towards me, yet I remained calmly on the arm of the couch (arguing) and Haney remained on the opposite end of the couch (not far from me). I sensed that he had no intentions of doing anything except intimidating me with his loud voice. Haney angrily advised, "Man, you better get your ass back down to that O.D. office and leave me the fuck alone!!" Now I stare Haney straight in the eye and questioned, "Nooo! And if I don't go down to the O.D. office, are you gonna kick my ass!!?" Haney, "I just want you to get your ass out of here!!" Author: "You need to understand one thing, I'm not one of your peers who you tell what to do, and they jump up and do it. I'll go when I want to go and I'll do what I want to do!!" Covering both ears with his fingers, Haney remarked, "Ok, fuck you man, but I'm not listenin' to you." Then Haney stared out the window as if to ignore me. Acknowledging that I was not very successful with Haney and further escalating the situation, I thought it best to leave. I left in frustration remarking, "deal with him Jim."

I left Jim to counsel Haney while I continued to walk through dorms. Coming out of Z-dorm I noticed Venessa (X-dorm counselor) and Duran walking away from X-dorm towards the pool (as if she wanted to take Duran away from X-dorm, i.e., take a break from the dorm and its chaos).

Again, a similar response structure is evident within this panic button encounter. Initially, there is discovery of the crisis, followed by a staff response. The staff response may range from charging to the scene, to restraint, to standing between two combatants, to isolating one resident in a secluded area. But what of restraint and isolation? How do staff use these acts to their advantage, thereby restoring order? Most OBH crises involve some type of restraint of residents by staff, which is observed by an audience of residents. Restraining residents in emergency situations is the only condition staff may legitimately "touch" residents in a forceful manner. Staff clearly stretch the physical nature of restraining residents, for residents often complain of irritating grabs, grips or holds. But it is within these situations where staff could "legitimately" abuse restrain holds, causing harm to residents. Like police officers, fellow OBH line staff are likely to overlook "illegitimate" restraint holds as part of their control. Clearly, panic buttons that require restraint become opportunities for staff to stretch the legitimacy of restraint holds, given that the situation justifies the restraint.

The issue of isolation is also relevant here. That is, X-dorm day room is a public area, thus isolating and questioning Haney there was counter productive in that it appeared he was responding to how he wanted other residents to view him. In short, we were in his territory. Though Duran was in another room, the saga continued because Haney retained his captive audience. By changing stages, from the day room to X-dorm office, there was less of an audience. Here, behind closed doors, staff became more challenging towards Haney in an effort to get at the bottom-line and solve the problem. Though we moved from the day room to the office, the audience really became myself and Jim. And when we frowned at his performance (his story), he became further enraged, directing his anger towards the O.D. I viewed Haney as attempting to establish an image by using residents and staff. We were less concerned about his image and more interested in protecting Duran and restoring control; but all (staff and residents) were used as props in the making of his image. So we did as much to remove the props, including myself, to restore order.

False Alarms

While there are two panic buttons in each dorm, one in the hallway and dorm office, alarms should only be activated by staff. The exception is when staff are physically unable, therefore directing a resident to "pull the panic button!" The hallway alarms are uncovered, making them most burdensome, because, while residents are instructed not to touch (or pull) the panic button, and are sanctioned if caught, it is difficult to continuously control and monitor the hallway. As one might expect, the hallway button is periodically pulled by residents, and explanations vary from accident, curiosity to an intentional rule violation.

Another dynamic of emergencies then, are false alarms. Such alarms hold a similar response structure as legitimate alarms, i.e., charging to the scene; yet when realized, false alarms produce emotions of relief and lessened anxiety. Relief, in that staff do not undergo the physical and mental energy necessary to stabilize emergencies. Too many false alarms may lead to frustrations by those responding to such alarms and negative evaluations of those whose dorms from which false alarms emanate. Additionally, there is a type of frustration expressed by staff who are victimized by residents covertly activating the alarm. Staff believe that residents intentionally pull alarms to witness the excitement and energy of staff responding to alarms. Staff have internalized a response pattern, therefore making certain assumptions when alarms are sounded. One does not discover an alarm being false until arrival on the scene.[5] Consequently, some staff believe that false alarms function as decoys for other delinquent activity by residents. The sociology of false alarms contains the dynamics of anomie (i.e., there is the question of "what's going on?"), relief, possible frustration and usually some sort of evaluation.

The dynamic of anomie appears present in every false alarm. Staff truly do not know "what's going on!" The ringing of the panic button signals certain assumptions to pursuing and on-site staff alike. When emergency assumptions do not materialize, then questions of "what's going on?" and "who pulled the panic button?" are raised to clear up confusion. In the case of X-dorm, there were two panic buttons that sounded back to back. That is, after resolving a legitimate emergency and stabilizing the situation by removing a resident (McDowell) to another dorm, the X-dorm alarm sounded again before anyone (staff) could settle and gather themselves:

> ...Before we could settle, X-dorm panic button rang a second time. Again, all staff (Claude of Y-dorm; Dio of W-dorm; Kara of Z-dorm; Bobby of V-dorm; Arnie and Jimmy from the night staff) responded. We were unclear as to who pulled the panic button, but we went storming down to X-dorm. I assumed Venessa (X-dorm counselor) pulled it. Venessa thought we (in the O.D. office) pulled it, assuming that McDowell (resident) had gotten away from us and rushed to X-dorm. This was not the case, and there was an exchange between myself and X-dorm staff (Venessa & Evia) regarding "who pulled the panic button?" Evia reasoned, "Either you pulled it or the kids are playing games with us." Author, "Yeah, the kids are playing games; they like to see us runnin' around." While we were in the X-dorm office, I told staff that possibly a resident pulled the button in the hallway. Evia then went yelling and screaming down the hall, "who pulled the panic button!!!?" No one responded, so she demanded,

"O.K., everybody in group!!! Get in group!!!"

Though residents grudgingly went to group, the purpose was to uncover the individual responsible. Moreover, staff's outrage led them to "call group" at a very odd and uncomfortable hour, e.g., 9:30pm, when most residents had been in bed and/or near sleep. So staff, in part, clearly wanted residents to feel their annoyance, even though the culprit was not discovered. "Calling group" was also a strategy to formally address the dynamics and problems of false alarms. Ultimately, the staff desired to confront the situation, thereby exerting a certain measure of competence and power over the covert action.

The next two examples show how staff are clearly unaware that an alarm is sounding. This lack of knowledge could lead to a humiliating experience (for staff) and damaging evaluations. Given that staff are in charge of dorms, they are expected to know that an emergency alarm, e.g., panic button, is sounding in their dorm. But the element of surprise, and to some degree embarrassment, meets with dorm staff who is unaware of an alarm--as the approaching staff arrive in the dorm:

> The panic button was set-off in Z-dorm and staff went runnin'. It sounded shortly before dinner. As I and other staff (William, Ricardo, Rob, Claude, Jen) ran towards Z-dorm, Claude yelled out, "Which dorm is it!?" Phil shouted back, "Z-dorm!" When we arrived, Terri-Ann (Z-dorm counselor) was in the office with the new psychiatrist, talking. The psychiatrist was sitting and Terri-Ann rushed to the office door to see why staff was rushing her dorm. She was unaware that the panic button had sounded. We asked, "what's going on!?" Terri-Ann, "Nothing." Rob, "Did you know your panic button was going off?" Terri-Ann looks down both ends of the hallway, then responds, "No." I then told her to "turn it off," and all staff returned to their respective dorms.

> The panic button sounded in W-dorm and as usual, staff rushed to the scene. When I arrived, W-dorm staff (Claude & Melis) and residents were in the hallway. W-dorm staff looked at the ensuing staff as if to ponder, 'what's going on? What are you doing down here.' Staff in turn responded to their facial gestures of surprise, asking, "What's goin' on?!! Your panic button is going off!!" Claude and Melis looked at each other puzzled, then Claude explained, "It didn't go off down here!! Did it go off in the office?" In the meantime, more staff (Rob & Evia) were arriving in W-dorm, Rob trips over a stone upon entry and embarrassingly inquires, "What are you

guys tryin' to do? Set booby traps in here." Next, the ensuing staff turned to check the office and we observed W-dorm social worker talking on the phone as if nothing had happened. Realizing that it was a false alarm, I turned and announced to the incoming staff, "it's a false alarm!" Melisa and Claude's faces were blank with embarrassment and speechless, for they did not know who pulled the panic button, nor were they aware that it was sounding.

Staff receiving the false alarm may appear incompetent in view of the approaching staff. That is, when asked, "what's goin' on?" the receiving staff are not aware, consequently they give no direction or instruction to approaching staff. Such staff members are often labeled "weak" and viewed as "not very dependable" during emergencies. Approaching staff then informs receiving staff by inquiring and discovering that the alarm is faulty (then move to silence it). Clearly the element of surprise is evident when examining facial gestures, body language and verbal expressions. This surprise is an indication of staff's honest ignorance regarding their lack of alarm awareness. Too much "honest ignorance" (too many false alarms) may result in response frustrations by approaching staff and slower responses by staff. That is, rather than "dropping everything" and rushing to the scene, staff have lingered by completing currents task (phone calls, giving medication, writing incident reports, watching a segment of a T.V. program) then making their way to the emergency site. In short, a certain doubt surfaces regarding the staff's ability when too many false alarms occur.

Evaluating Staff Use of the Panic Button

The panic button is met with mixed reviews by staff. Some staff believe it is over used, misused and therefore abused. Other staff consider it a crutch for weak staff, and staff's response to panic buttons unduly excites residents. Whatever the reasons, there is little agreement on the panic button usage; consequently, the panic button has lost its response urgency by staff over time.

Through observation and experience, staff have become socialized regarding how they will actually respond.[6] That is, the social evaluation of staff when responding to panic buttons has caused various staff to hesitate when sounding the alarm, and still others simply refuse to respond to the panic button, if they can "swing" it. For example, Garr Tays (recreation staff) boasted, "I don't respond to panic buttons because it's not my job. I remember one time when I was standing in the gym door and the panic button rang. I saw Phil Simmons (Z-dorm social worker) talking to Mr. Nash (Executive Director). When the panic button rang, Phil shot up to X-dorm. I said 'damn!!' To me, it looked like he was puttin' on a show for Mr. Nash." Clearly, in the face of the executive director, one is likely to over-emphasize a panic button response. Phil may well have demonstrated his competence by his response strategy thus "showing" he too was concerned about the smooth operation of the Home.

Meanwhile, Don Benton appears far more hesitant to use the panic button than other staff. Consider our conversation:

> Don Benton called me (O.D.) down to Z-dorm because a resident had barricaded himself in his room. By the time I arrived, Don had calmed and dealt with the situation. In fact, the room door was open and Don was talking to this resident. When I arrived, Don and I spoke in the hallway outside of this resident's room. Don mentioned that "this dorm has been crazy all night." Author, "well why didn't you pull the panic button?" Don laughs and says, "Oh no, I try to avoid the panic button as much as I can. The staff (Joanita & Davy) was tellin' me to 'pull the panic button, pull the panic button.' But I said 'no.' I didn't want all those staff running down here just to see this guy barricaded in his room."

Don's perception of the incident was not very serious, and therefore assumed that other staff would view it as minor. He sought to avoid "all those staff running down here" observing and resolving an incident that Z-dorm staff could solve. In short, Don decided against using the panic button because he did not want other staff "to see this guy barricaded in his room"; and possibly to avoid a potential escalation that the response of other staff would bring.

Moreover, Don is illustrating that there are alternatives to the panic button as ways to de-escalate and resolve emergencies. Don called (by phone) the O.D. for assistance, Brenie (staff) broke up a fight along with help from residents, and Trib (staff) counseled Bright (resident) after breaking a window. In Brenie's case:

> "Brandon (resident) put a cat into Robert's (resident) face, Robert attempted to hit Brandon, staff intervened. Brandon (resident) said

something to Robert. Robert charged at Brandon attempting to hit him. Brandon attempted to charge back at Robert, staff and residents prevented the residents from hitting each other. Derrik (resident) attempted to agitate both boys into a physical altercation by laughing at them and saying, 'you guys aren't going to fight, you ain't tough.'"

In Trib's case:

"All residents were told by staff to line up for rec. (recreation) time in the gym. Residents were not lining up properly, so were told to go to their rooms (the dorm is on closure at this time). Gerald became very upset when told to return to his room. He ran to his room (room six) and immediately punched out a windowpane with his right fist. Staff immediately counseled with him until he appeared calm and in control of his behavior..."

In the previous three cases, staff could have clearly activated the panic button but chose otherwise. Some staff use other control methods, including the use of residents, before alerting external dorm staff that a severe problem exist and assistance is needed. Pulling panic buttons invites external staff to assist in resolving crises, asking questions and becoming knowledgeable of dorm problems. But using alternative methods minimizes knowledge gained by outsiders concerning internal problems, thus lessening external evaluations. Alternative methods further suggest attainment of certain control skills and knowledge that novice or "weak" staff have yet to achieve.

On the other hand, there are certain staff members who abuse the panic button by using it too loosely and too frequently. Instead of finding an alternative method, certain staff are heavily dependent on the panic button. Venessa and Malik (X-dorm staff) sounded the panic button because Mitchell (resident) refused to "get off the phone." When staff arrived, Mitchell was off the phone and Venessa was arguing with him as he was leaving the staff office. But there was little perceived danger to staff or residents, so arriving staff looked strangely at each other as to imply, "why would she use the panic button for this?" then returned to our respective areas.

Claude and Ben often used the panic button too frequently, and usually when working alone. They gained a reputation of using the panic button for "every little thing." Claude has used the panic button for fights between residents, arguments between residents, poor line-ups, and residents who verbally threaten staff. Ben has similarly use the panic button in cases of "I heard noises outside" the dorm, fights between residents, residents trying to get into the awol closet without permission, "extreme disruptiveness" in group, and tampering with the dorm fire extinguisher. While certain usages are legitimate, the frequency (i.e., three times in one night, or three times during a weekend shift) of using the panic button begins to tax the urgency of staff respond. Even though the alarm is legitimate, certain staff response is slower. Not to mention other staff begin to question the abilities of Claude and Ben in that certain staff wish to ignore Claude and Ben because, according to Shari, "I have my own problems; and I don't pull the panic button for every little thing!!" Don Benton maintained, "the reason he (Claude) pulls the panic button so much is because he's a wimpy staff and the kids know they can take advantage of him. How many times have I pulled the panic button?" His anxious personality is another reason for staff irritation with Claude. During panic button responses, Claude is often observed yelling at residents, telling the resident in question that "I want you out of my dorm" or "I want him to go to juvenile hall," without checking and consulting with the proper OBH officials. Staff cannot arbitrarily send residents to juvenile hall without "hall clearance." Nor can they place residents in another dorm unless spaces are available.

At OBH, there exist a sentiment that staff should be able to handle certain problems without using the panic button, and maintain composure when dealing with minor problems. Abusing the panic button by using it too loosely or too frequently raises questions, among staff, about "carrying staff", that is, it raises questions about staff's ability to perform their tasks. Moreover, Dave Benton contends that staff who cannot "carry their weight" probably should not hold their position, for one staff must do the work of two. This is a source of alienation and discontent among staff, which could therefore lead to a decline in staff morale.

Additionally, Mara and Phil contend that P.A.R.T. has spawned an overly aggressive staff when responding to panic buttons. Mara declared that "too many staff respond to the panic button and this excites residents more. When I respond to the panic button and I see everything is under control, I back off." While staff response may effect residents, according to Mara, she further expressed that "some staff 'get off on' (really enjoy) responding to the panic button," blaming the newly required restraint course (P.A.R.T.) for such behavior.[7] In fact, Phil, social worker, concurs that the panic button has caused more physically aggressive behavior among staff. He confessed that "I've never seen so many fights; I never seen so many staff take down residents; I never seen so many staff hurt. I believe if you can't talk him down, you shouldn't be here."

While emergency systems are necessary, staff at OBH are in part suggesting that panic button procedures be refined. According to Mara and Phil, P.A.R.T. training has increased staff usage of emergency buttons and staff aggression. But solving one problem (staff efficiency in emergency response) has contributed to other problems, e.g. false alarms, staff injuries and abusing alarms. Given that P.A.R.T. training does teach staff how to restrain residents, staff seems more likely to solve a problem physically rather than verbally. Phil's preference is discussion and communication, for it is more conducive to treatment institutions; and if there were more emphasis on counseling, as a strategy to resolve conflict, then there may very well be less need to activate alarms, as well as an immediate use of restraint when arriving on the emergency scene.[8]

Summary

This chapter has addressed how control is done during emergency situations. When emergencies occur, the panic button is depressed; and staff typically "charge to the scene" in an effort to restore control. Yet before order is restored, staff must *get there* (to emergency location). Order is delayed and emergencies may take on a different character, when staff are slowed in *getting there!!* So rushing to the scene and *getting there* are significant to controlling the situation. And while *there*, staff will do whatever is necessary to re-establish control.

False alarms are another dynamic tied to institutional emergencies. Such alarms contain a similar response structure; yet when realized, false alarms produce emotions of relief and frustration. Moreover, the sociology of false alarms contains the dynamics of anomie and usually some sort of evaluation. The feeling of anomie raises the question of "what's going on?" And, too many false alarms may lead to frustrations by those responding to such alarms and negative evaluations of those whose dorms from which false alarms emanate.

Finally, evaluating staff use of the panic button is met with mixed reviews. That is, some staff believe that panic buttons are over used, misused and abused. Other staff consider "buttons" a crutch for weak staff, and staff response to panic buttons unduly excites residents. Thus, alternatives to the panic button may prove advantageous. For example, pulling emergency buttons invites external staff to assist in resolving crises, asking questions and becoming knowledgeable of dorm problems. But using alternative methods minimizes knowledge gained by outsiders concerning internal problems, thus lessening external evaluations.

Notes

1. The panic button system was installed September 1987.

2. Panic buttons were installed in locations most likely to incur emergencies.

3. These policies are not always observed. Some staff believe that their residents are responsible & trustworthy enough to monitor themselves, thereby allowing staff to assist in the emergency. Other times, due to staffing shortages, there's a need to impose on one staff to monitor (cover) two dorms. Resource allocation is a common problem among institutions concerned with social control (See Robert M Emerson, "Holistic Effects in Social Control Decision-Making," *Law & Society Review*, 1983).

4. The "box" is a single detaining unit where unruly inmates (in juvenile hall) are placed. They remain there for an extended period of time, for example, from days to weeks. Here, their activity is isolated from other inmates.

5. The exception is when staff accidentally pull the panic button (by the string becoming attached to a office chair) then call the O.D. informing him of the error. The staff may have already silenced the alarm, but if not, the O.D. will instruct him to silence the alarm. Staff arriving at the O.D. office are told of the false alarm. But typically, alarms are discovered upon arrival, and staff inform other pursuing staff of the false nature of the alarm.

6. Unlike fire drills, there has never been a formal run-through or actual practice, among staff, as to how one should respond to the panic button.

7. See chapter on "Learning Control" to review P.A.R.T. training.

8. A comparison of OBH staff and police officers proves quite interesting when examining attitudes towards responding to emergencies. At times, OBH staff

appear impersonal and indifferent, possessing an "I'll be there when I can, If I can" attitude. At other times, certain "staff 'get off on responding to the panic button.'" But for police officers, they appear more loyal and cohesive, thus viewing themselves as family. That is, "police officers often remark that one of the most cherished aspects of their occupation is the spirit of 'one for all, and all for one.'" (Bittner, 1974:237). According to Ahern (1972), the "closed fraternity" developed by policemen help to shape informal norms, privileges and expectations that come with being a member. At OBH, there is no such fraternity, nor is there a spirit of "one for all, and all for one." Yet there is the sense that one should respond when panic buttons are activated (even though OBH staff do not express loyalty in emergencies and often cite problems with the emergency system). Police seem to respond more out of brotherhood and obligation, whereas OBH staff are driven by expectations of the occupation.

Chapter 6

Resident Leaving: Awoling

Awols and terminations focus on "leaving" the facility, either voluntarily or involuntarily. Awols indicate that residents leave without permission, while residents who are terminated are forced to leave. Both may return and many do, but "resident leaving" appears to temporarily relieve staff of inappropriate and sometimes nerve-racking behavior by residents. Those residents who graduate[1] are perceived as successfully leaving, yet a negative stigma is attached to residents who awol or terminate. Thus, I explore the sociological significance of leaving (e.g., awoling and termination) an enclosed semi-total institution.

For staff, "leaving" is a very important control tool. Residents who do not wish to conform or despise detention may leave, e.g., awol. Although awoling violates a resident's court order, "leaving" may assist staff in better control of dorms. Eventually, most awolees (residents who awol) return, giving staff more leverage over the resident's behavior and future at OBH. Returning awolees who fail or refuse to adhere to program standards are ultimately terminated. The resident's behavior (awoling, refusing to follow program expectations) determines the type of control options used by staff. Termination, or sending residents to juvenile hall is the harshest and final instance of control available to staff. In short, if all else fails, termination is the last control option.

Deciding to Awol

The open structure of OBH seems inviting and tempting for residents who contemplate awoling. For instance, OBH is an open facility which has no entrance gate that opens and closes as employees and visitors come and go. Typically, the dorm's entrance doors and room doors remain unlock, while most room windows freely open and close. Staff, on the other hand, must report an awol but they are not required to physically prevent residents from leaving. So, the OBH structure is conducive for awoling if residents desire.[2]

Given the physical and social structure of OBH, awoling could be a most difficult situation to control; that is, difficult when staff desire residents to stay rather than leave. The most effective control style is staff's ability to convince residents that awoling is unwise. Thus depending on the resident or staff's relationship with certain residents determines whether staff will attempt to reverse the resident's awol decision or in some way, urge him to leave. On the other hand, the "Home" is psychologically designed to keep residents there. That is, violating a court order (awoling) and getting caught or turning oneself in—could result in additional punishments. Moreover, the "home atmosphere" (as opposed to juvenile hall) and amenities connected to OBH are difficult to resist. In short, doing time in a community-base facility becomes bearable; there is a certain autonomy attached to OBH that is not evident in juvenile hall. Staff frequently convey to residents that residential treatment is a privilege, given the numerous juveniles attempting and awaiting placement (admission). Violating one's court order (awoling) indicates that residents wish to be elsewhere. Thus, there are psychological, social and punitive control mechanism built into suppressing one's desire to leave.

While OBH is not a concentration camp or prison, residents do obtain the urge to leave. Resident escapes are not as dramatic as prisoner's, but some residents do attempt to outwit authority by leaving at night through rear room windows, or by constructing dummies and placing them underneath their bed covers in an attempt to deceive staff regarding their presence. This chapter then examines how residents awol, and staff responses to resident awols.

Staff responses to resident awols have implications for the overall fate of awolees who return to OBH. That is, staff do not make uniform responses to resident awols; in fact, their reactions vary from "it depends" to a punitive "lock 'em up and throw away the key." The decision to awol may be spontaneous or well thought through but leaving without permission (awoling) is a violation of OBH policy and the resident's court order. Additionally, residents who awol are defying an institutional rule, which could lead to grave consequences, e.g. termination.

As mentioned earlier, awol reports are formal organizational documents on which staff use to report resident awols. One section of this awol report requires that staff explain the "circumstances surrounding awol." Here staff indicate several reasons for resident awols; some of which include threatening staff, suspicious about being terminated to juvenile hall, experiencing night problems, smoking marijuana, smoking cigarettes in unauthorized areas, stealing, vandalism, on grounds awol (OGA), and an overall frustration with Opportunity Boys' Home. On the one hand, staff may quote a frustrated resident who leaves in a rage, claiming, "I didn't break that fuckin' window." On the other, staff may construct awol explanations by asking residents and/or staff to reveal residential awol reasons. Staff however are expected to provide an awol explanation, recognizing that each resident who awols makes a conscious choice to leave.[3] Finally, knowing that staff are required to document awols, essentially, they are constructing their interpretation of how and why residents awol.

Awol Types

"Awol types" addresses how staff construct residential awols. I have developed "awol types" to assist in understanding "common threads" among similar categories and making clear distinctions among others. Gibbons (1994:59) argues that "when we sort offenders into behavioral types, we invent conceptual schemes that allow us to see common threads or characteristics that identify groups of similar offenders." Developing typologies are nothing new for social scientist; for instance, Irwin (1970) Conklin (1972), Glaser (1972) and Gibbons (1992) all created typologies or classifications to aid them in analyzing, grouping and distinguishing between types.[4] This same idea is apparent when constructing "awol types"; it simply permits better explanations of a general phenomenon (awoling).

Generally, there are five types of awols experienced by residents, e.g., **injustice awols, terminal awols, avoidance awols, lonesome awols** and **sneaky thrills** (Katz, 1988) **awols. Injustice awols** refer to residents who awol as protest against penalties they claim they did not deserve. **Terminal awols** are those that residents chose to awol rather than terminate to juvenile hall. **Avoidance awols** are those which seek to avoid sanctions for rule infractions, like fighting, smoking marijuana, threatening staff, fighting staff, stealing, OGA, etc. **Lonesome awols** are experienced by residents who have not socially interacted with girlfriends or family members for weeks, months, and sometimes years; there is an emotional longing for love ones. Finally, there is a certain excitement and boldness generated by **sneaky thrill awols**.

"Awol types" are developed from accounts and excuses given by residents for awoling. Residents provide accounts and excuses to staff upon their return. Other times, awol accounts and excuses are acquired before residential departures, as in the case of Brown.[5] Residents give awol accounts to convey images of themselves and their situation. At times, awol accounts are little more than defenses and rationalizations for residential (awol) behavior. Staff then receive these accounts, constructing their version of residential awols. Hence, as staff interact with residents who awol or those who have awol knowledge, we begin to see how the awol construction process unfolds, eventually becoming a formal document, i.e., awol report.

One reason OBH residents awol is because of a perceived sense of **injustice**, causing various residents to "get tired of this fuckin' place." There is the sense that I have been treated unfairly though I have done nothing wrong. "Getting tired of this fuckin' place" suggest certain coping limits for residents. That is, some residents who are free of personal "troubles" might suffer from a negative dorm environment and opt out. Garcia, for example, revealed that he was experiencing no personal problems, e.g., "I wasn't in trouble. I didn't get in trouble or nothing, I just took off." In the same conversation, Garcia conveyed that the chaotic dorm environment, which led to a collective sanction, was instrumental in his leaving. Consider our conversation:

> O.D.: why did you leave? Garcia: No man, 'cause in group and shit man, we got put on close for people messin' up and shit; and I was all pissed off 'cause I wasn't even messin' up. 'Cause I was on one of the highest status, I got pissed off, you know, I said fuck it, you know. People were tryin' to put me down and shit, you know like I ain't doing good and shit like that, you know. So, I just got pissed off and took off.

While the structure of OBH is conducive to awoling, there are other structural factors that alienate residents, which could provoke their leaving. Garcia's reference to "we got put on close" suggests that certain residents of his dorm were delinquent, resulting in a collective sanction. Dorm closure is a condition that strips or limits *all* residents of dorm, OBH and individual privileges and activities. For example, residents scheduled for weekend home passes may be denied; outings and field trips are eliminated or postponed; video and T.V. viewing is curbed; bedtime is earlier; phone calls are denied or seriously restricted; group sessions could last all day; and staff surveillance is tighter. Apparently, Garcia felt this punishment (dorm closure) was unfair because he had nothing to do with the chaotic nature of the dorm that caused it to close.

Consequently, another structural factor contributing to resident estrangement, which could lead to awoling, is a pessimistic attitude by staff toward residents. At times, staff need an emotional and physical break from residents, but unable to take such a break. Staff communication of this desired "break" maybe cynical and rude. Additionally, staff might be unconcerned about a resident's problems, yet such problems are quite significant to residents. If staff fails to fully investigate a resident who is accused of stealing and the resident is thereby sanctioned though later found "innocent," a feeling of unfairness could emerge, leading the resident to awol. Finally, a resident playing his radio too loud may cause *all* radios to be confiscated, e.g., a collective sanction to an individual act. Collective sanctions generate perceptions of unjustified punishment from those uninvolved. These situations, then, may cause residents to receive a feeling that the institution is closing in on them, therefore seek release or temporary escape through awoling.

When residents chose **terminal awols**, they seem to convey an unwillingness to return to juvenile hall, risking any possibility of returning to OBH, and becoming a fugitive. Lackey (resident) is a case in point, in that, upon discovering his termination to juvenile hall rather than transitioning home, he decided to flee. According to Don (staff), he and Ricardo (staff) walked Lackey out to the van, but Lackey claimed that he wanted to return to the dorm to get some clothes. Don granted Lackey permission. But when Lackey returned, he was carrying his packed bags, refused to get in the van and go to juvenile hall, and walked out the front gate. Don expressed dismay because he felt that Lackey should have been uninformed of his termination. Janis (Z-dorm social worker) informed

Lackey, and Don said aloud, "You should never tell these guys that you're takin' 'em to the hall." By knowing of their termination, staff assume that residents will in some way resist, and possibly steal property of other residents (usually roommate).

Maldanodo is another who awoled because of terminal conditions. Consider his explanation:

> Author, "Why did you awol?" Maldanodo, "'Cause I thought I was gonna be terminated." Author, "So why did you come back?" Maldanodo, "'Cause I found out that they were not gonna terminate me." Author, How'd you find out?" Maldanodo, "Jiminez (Maldanodo awoled with Jiminez and Ponce; all assumed they would be terminated) called and asked if he could come back, but they (staff) said he was terminated. Then they (staff on the phone) asked about me and Ponce. Jiminez said he didn't know where we were, but they (staff) told him to tell us to come back."

The extent to which residents want to leave OBH is debatable, but it is clear that they do not wish to terminate to juvenile hall. If given a second chance, some will return. Maldanodo returned because "they were not gonna terminate me." Jiminez remained truant due to his termination status. Given that Jiminez made the call, it is quite likely that he too would have returned had his status been reverse. But awoling to avert termination is a reality for some residents; they don't accept the oft stated counsel and advice by staff, e.g., going to juvenile hall gives residents a higher probability of returning to OBH, failure to do so greatly reduce their chances.

Unlike Garcia, Lackey and Maldanodo, Morrison (white resident) was experiencing individual troubles and decided to leave. His awol, resulting from a drug involvement, is an exemplary case of **avoidance**. Consider the source:

> Morrison awoled because he was accused of a drug involvement, e.g., apparently he planted a marijuana pipe in the awol closet. According to Morrison, Mandy (W-dorm supervisor) thinks he planted the pipe so W-dorm residents could not go on their scheduled camping trip. W-dorm did go camping.
>
> According to Dio (W-dorm counselor), a pipe was found in W-dorm's small awol closet (where clothes from awolees are kept). Dio, "I smelled Morrison's fingers and they smelled like marijuana. Then I told him to

empty his pants pockets but he refused and left."

Morrison returned from awol before W-dorm returned from their camping trip (he stayed in V-dorm); however, upon W-dorm's return, the marijuana issue was still alive and it was discussed in group. According to Dio, Morrison left again because of the marijuana pipe, "he could not take responsibility for it."

Morrison leaves because he does not wish to deal with the issue (drug involvement), nor does he desire hassling by staff. The smell of marijuana on Morrison's fingers is strong evidence of his drug involvement; and refusal to empty pockets, implies that Morrison is hiding something? Might the marijuana be in his pocket? No one knows, but what we do know is that he left, and when he returned he was more willing to be searched. That is, during the second awol return, I recorded the following:

> During my questioning, Morrison stood in the doorway of the O.D. office. He later came in when he was searched. I basically requested that he search himself, that is, take off his shoes and socks, empty his pockets, un-cuff his pants, etc. Here he was very cooperative. I then sent him to W-dorm were Dio resumed questioning.

Regarding Morrison's initial awol, is it possible that he disposed the marijuana while awol? Is this why he returns and is more cooperative?[6] Was he avoiding the immediate sanction of the drug involvement, and possibly the actual evidence of the drug itself. When later confronted during group about the marijuana, Morrison leaves again. Why? It appears he does not wish to deal with it, and hassling from staff. But there is strong evidence (the smell of his fingers) as to why he avoids emptying his pocket(s), which heightens the suspicion, and why he avoids discussing the drug involvement during group. Morrison's handling of these situations suggests that he was somehow involved.

Additionally, a group of residents (Wilson, Dorsey, Banks, Cuevas and Loza) awoled because they were confronted by staff for smoking in the day room during a forbidden time. According to Chara (X-dorm counselor), they were smoking during staff meeting and "some were smoking in the bathroom of room eight." These residents left to avoid further confrontation, immediate counsel and sanction. Here residents are often running away from troubles; troubles that they are not willing to face, and sometimes, admit to or accept responsibility. Avoidance awol is often a reaction to a condition or situation, e.g., smoking, fighting, OGA, etc. And while it is true that some residents are not involved, they awol to avoid the atmosphere of accusation, e.g., "I don't want to deal with it!"

Lonesome awols indicate an emotional longing for love ones, namely girlfriends and family members. In such cases, residents are not clearly focused on improving their programs but they appear preoccupied in contacting love ones. Improving their program does not seem to matter, at the moment. However, after seeing love ones, their interest in improving behavior tends to take shape, and love ones play roles in their improved behavioral progress.

When Dominguez (resident) returned from awol, I asked, "Why'd you leave?" "I wanted to see my girlfriend," Dominguez said. "How long have you been here?" Dominguez, "Since last Thursday." "How long were you in the Hall?" As he stands in front of me, Dominguez appears very honest and cooperative, remarking, "A month-and-a-half." Now I am puzzled about his girlfriend response, inquiring, "So you haven't seen your girl-friend in a month-and-a-half and you awoled to see her?!!" Dominguez: "No, I haven't seen her since March.[7] I was in another placement before I went to the Hall." Now that the girlfriend issue is made clear, I'm wondering, "Why did you come back?" Dominguez appeared quite sincere in his response, "Because my girlfriend wanted me too and because it'd be easier."

Another lonesome resident could not effectively concentrate on his program because he had not seen or heard from his grandmother. Even on return, Evans (resident) remained depressed, that is his head was partially bowed as he drug his feet through the O.D. entrance door. Consider our encounter:

> "Why did you leave?" Evans, "They (staff) would not let me go home, because they couldn't get in touch with my grandmother." Author, "Did you find her?" Evans, "Yes." Author, "What did you do while you were out there?" Evans, "I just stayed with my grandmother." There is a moment of silence. Then I asked, "Where else did you go?" Evans, "Over some friends." Author, "How'd you decide to come back?" Evans, "Because everything was alright with my grandmother." "What about your mother," I asked? "She died," said Evans.

Lonesome awols reflect a longing for a familiar and comforting companion, someone that residents trust with thoughts and personal belongings. Returning from awol, Garcia expressed, "I needed someone to talk to bad; someone I can trust and stuff. Talk to one of the staff, you know. But its like when you talk to one of them, you talk to them all. But when you talk to your parents, they sit down and listen and shit, and they help you." In part, lonesome awols reflects a type of need that residents possess to be near love ones who do not hold their faults and delinquent record against them. Such love ones know their personal and social history, good and bad, though accept them for who they are and who they are trying to become, recognizing potential in their character and ability.

Finally, there is the **sneaky thrills awol** where residents may go through elaborate mechanisms (constructing dummies, using back windows after midnight, informing certain residents of their scheduled departure, departing behind dorm or climbing fences) to conceal their escape. The function of elaborate mechanisms is to trick staff; and fooling staff is part of the thrill associated with this type of awol. Some residents however do not use elaborate mechanism, they are either curious or solely interested in having fun.

For example, when Wilson and Jones returned at 2am, Wilson stated that they wanted to "have a little fun." According to Wilson (resident), "We went walkin' around, uuh uhh, you know we went to the store, uh, we went to Safeway. We walked to Taco Bell. We ordered two burritos, (pause), and when they closed down we asked them to give us two free burritos, and they did." Author, "how'd you guys decide to come back?" Wilson, "we just wanted to get away for awhile, you know, have a little fun. We didn't want to stay away, we were gonna come back." Moreover, Trejo conveyed that he and a group of residents (Macias, Acuna, & Conners) awoled because they "wanted to get high." And finally, after a lengthy incarceration before coming to OBH, Trujillo seemed very curious as to "what was out there." He confessed, "I wanted to see what was out there, you know, what was going on in the streets, 'cause I haven't been out there in eleven months."

Sneaky thrills awols examines a type adolescent excitement and boldness that transcends everyday routines. There is a willingness to take an exciting risk—just for the fun of it. Such thrills and risks may provide an underground status that elevates residents to leaders and consultants among other would-be thrill seekers. It is a type of awol that everyone is not brave enough to experience. So part of the thrill is returning and telling (or over-telling) staff and residents what they experienced; and making it sound worthwhile, given the sanctions they face. These same residents may awol again, just for the thrill of it; and through their talk, recruit others who become curious about what they hear. Still others who hear the exciting talk about awoling may feel pressure, by an underground subculture, to participate next time.

Awols: Detection, Non-Detection

Awols are analyzed in two broad categories, e.g., detection, and non-detection. Given that each awol is situationally unique, careful consideration must be taken of each category. That is, there are variations within in each category, making generalizations difficult.

The first category concerns awols staff detect before they occur, e.g., detection. The various stages are detection, negotiation, decision, and documentation. In the following section ("Process of Awoling"), I present three cases where staff are on the front end of **detection**; but within each case, there is of course variation. The Brown and Duran cases concern **negotiation**, but the quality of negotiation is quite distinct. For example, negotiation with Duran (and to a lesser extent Pendleton, who considers awoling with Duran) addresses his **decision** to "stay or go." In short, they are presented a choice. Brown however, does not receive this same type of choice. Actually, Brown begins negotiating the possibility of "staying" or remaining in placement. That is, he attempts to negotiate a choice, e.g., another chance. Here Brown's choice becomes terminal in that he may awol or terminate to juvenile hall; he is forced to make a choice. Finally, Mata's awol shows no negotiation, but simply makes his decision.

In other detection cases, negotiation may occur but some staff members are indifferent about the resident's options, as in the Duran and Pendleton case. When I discovered that Duran and Pendleton were considering awol, I impatiently demanded to know their plans, e.g., "O.K. what's goin' on? Are you guys gonna awol or are you gonna stay here? If you're gonna awol, go! If you're gonna stay, go to bed! But you cannot stay up, that's one thing you cannot do." Alternatively, there are times when staff attempt to dissuade awols, while on others, some staff encourage leaving. For instance, Raymond (staff) was overjoyed when Taylor (resident) left. Raymond smiled, grinding from "ear to ear," as he reported Taylor's awol:

The O.D. asked, "Taylor left, right?" Raymond's smile enlarges as he sits in a chair across from the O.D. desk, then with his Spanish accent, comments, "Body language, see my face (pointing to his smiling face). No, some guys I really try to work with and try to talk them out of awoling, but others, you can't pay them to leave. You drop a dollar and hope they get the hint but they won't go. I was happy to see Taylor leave. I called his mother and told her he was all 'blued down' (dressed in all blue gang clothing, crip colors). His mother said he (Taylor) called her and said he was coming home. You know, it's that gang stuff; he'll probably get hurt out there."

Eventually, a **decision** must be made. Duran and Pendleton will stay, but for Brown and Mata, the awol resolution seems more desirable than "the hall." Whether residents consider the consequences of their action is debatable. But it is fair to say, that both Duran and Brown will give critical thought to their actions.

Finally there is **documentation**. That is, whether residents awol or not staff must document the awol consideration. Actual awols are documented on awol reports, recorded in the main and dorm log and printed on a felt bulletin board behind the O.D. desk. Parents, police and probation officers are called and informed; police and probation officers eventually receive copies of awol reports. Awols that are considered but do not materialize are recorded in the dorm log only.

The non-detection category considers awols staff detect after the fact. It considers non-detection and documentation. That is, X-resident may inform staff that Y-resident left. Conversely, while doing a morning, noon or evening head count, staff discovers that Y-resident has awoled. Next, staff would attempt to uncover an awol reason by asking friends of the awolee, conducting group, or consulting another staff. If staff is unable to determine an awol reason, he simply writes "unknown" in the space provided on the awol report. As in the detection category, awol documentation and reporting remains the same where appropriate.

The Process of Awoling

Staff and residents interpret the process of awol quite differently. On many occasions, staff are able to observe and participate in the awol process. That is, while staff are prohibited from physically restraining residents who decide to awol, some staff may attempt to deter residents through counsel, e.g., "it would be best to stay and deal with your problems." Other staff are not necessarily interested in counseling or treatment, but enforcing institutional rules. That is, it does not matter where stray residents go or the strategy used to awol. What does matters is the *time* of awol, whether theft or vandalism occurs, and that residents actually leave OBH--which are all recorded on awol reports. Therefore, staff who are cognizant of residents awoling will most likely observe residents as they pack and leave to make a first hand report and prevent possible wrongdoings during awols.

Staff believe that residents are aware of the structure and treatment philosophy of OBH. Some staff therefore maintain that residents who are unhappy at OBH are free to leave. Staff recognize however, that leaving is not as "easy" as it appears, in that many residents do contemplate the consequences of their actions. An awolee returning from awol may be stripped of all privileges, receive a status drop, graduation date postponed, terminated to juvenile hall, etc. While penalties are situationally subjective, the quantity of awols and character of residents are considered. But the lack of an objective sanction for awoling as well as inconsistency in sanctions contributes to one's increased willingness to awol. That is, when residents awol, then return and receive minimal "sentencing," other residents may contemplate awoling, anticipating minor sanctions. Various staff contend that applying minimal "sentencing" to returnees sends inconsistent messages to residents and circumvents staff ability to control.

The awol process guides us through the various steps of an awol as viewed by staff. The first to discover missing residents, may or may not be staff but the method of departure seems to reveal a certain disposition (anxious, worried, indifferent, rational) of residents and their message(s) sent to OBH community. Residents who awol just prior to graduation are viewed by staff as having second thoughts about leaving OBH. And while residents brag about graduating and being on the "outs", their awol behavior seems to indicate a certain fear of "independence." Staff reasons that if a resident awols five days before graduating, it is his way of conveying that he is not ready to leave, or he is afraid of graduating. Hence, staff believe that residents are communicating some type of message whenever they awol.

The next three instances carry us through the awol process as viewed, interpreted and recorded by staff. The conditions that lead to awols are distinctive in each case. The first case examines Duran's (resident) attempt to deceive staff by placing a stuffed dummy in his bed. The second instance examines how two staff react after driving Mata (resident) to San Bernarndino juvenile hall and helplessly watch him awol. The final awol explores staff responses to a threatening resident and his decision to awol rather than do time in juvenile hall. The purpose of these instances is to illustrate the experiences of staff as they interact with residents (awolees) during an awol. What is an awol like? And exactly what does staff do during an awol?

The Duran Case

Upon checking out, I (O.D.) walked down through X-dorm to inform Shorty (night staff) that I was leaving. As I approached X-dorm, walking through the day room and dim hallway, I noticed Pendleton (resident) stick his head out of room seven. Seeing Pendleton, I assumed he was looking for staff. But as we eyed each other, Pendleton ducked back into room seven. I passed X-dorm office before reaching room seven; my intentions were simply to quickly make my presence known to Robert and then, check on Pendleton, since he was up. But when I showed my face in X-dorm office doorway, Shorty immediately reported, "We (Willis, new X-dorm counselor, sat across the desk from Shorty) just had a drug involvement." Laughingly, Shorty continued by pointing and placing his index finger on the desk mat to a very small portion of marijuana: "The evidence is right here." I did not completely enter the office; I remained in the doorway for I wanted to check on Pendleton. Shorty then remarked: "The bathroom really smelled strong." Before Shorty went any further, I interrupted Robert, saying "o.k." and walked down to investigate Pendleton.

Then I went to room seven where the door was open, room dark, and it appeared as though someone was underneath bed covers. That is, the two beds seemed occupied by residents sleeping. So I looked across the hall into room four where the door was open, the room was dark (lights out), but here, there were three beds and one was empty. I thought, "maybe the missing person was in the restroom," so I checked the restroom but it was empty. After coming out of the restroom, I yelled down the darkened hall for Willis, "Willis, Willis!!" No answer from Willis. So I tried again, a little louder this time, "Willis, Willis, Willis!!!" I did not move from this position, for I thought that going to the office would give the missing resident a chance to return to his proper place. After about fifteen seconds, the loud heater went off (apparently, the heater prevented Willis from hearing me initially) and I yelled for Willis again, "Willis, Willis!!" Willis and Shorty (Shorty walked behind Willis) came out of the office, walking towards myself. As Willis came closer, I asked as he stood outside of room four, "Who's in this room?" Peaking inside of room four, Willis answered, "Pendleton." Author, "Well where is he?" Willis, "I don't know, he's not here!" Author, "I know he's not here, but where's he at?" Willis, "I don't know!"

Willis, Shorty and I began our search for Pendleton. I walk straight into room seven, where it is darkened, though partially lit from the hallway light. I walk into the middle of the room where a bed is on either side. Then looking at the foot of the bed, which is closest to the entrance door, I noticed a foot, covered with a white sock. The foot was not underneath covers as the rest of the body. I looked towards the head of the bed and noticed the person's head was also covered. Thus, I pulled the covers off the individual to see who was underneath. I discovered the "person" was a dummy constructed by Duran (resident).

The apparent foot was a sock covering a tennis shoe, which stuck out and was attached to the pants leg; both pants legs were stuffed with clothes. The upper body (chest, back and abdomen area) was not well constructed. That is, there was no shirt stuffed with clothes; clothes were simply positioned and placed together in a way that produced a type of back.

I switched on the light and first noticed Pendleton, for he was hiding behind the closet, and hiding behind the room door was Duran. Both residents came out from hiding soon after the lights came on. Duran was fully dressed and it looked as though he was about to awol, Pendleton was fully dressed but he claimed that he was not going to awol. Staff Shorty and Willis soon entered. As Duran seemed to surrender (by sitting at the foot of the bed), he amusingly said to Willis, referring to his dummy, "Pretty good, uhh?" Laughing while responding, Willis agrees by saying, "Yeah, but it's not good enough because you got caught." Then I firmly address both residents, demanding, "O.K. what's goin' on? Are you guys gonna awol or are you gonna stay here? If you're gonna awol, go! If you're gonna stay, go to bed! But you cannot stay up, that's one thing you cannot do." Pendleton then speaks up, "I'm not gonna awol." I command, "Then you go to your room and go to bed!!!" Pendleton leaves with no problems. Looking at Duran, I restate my question, "Duran, what are you gonna do? Are you gonna awol or what!?" Duran, "I don't know what I'm gonna do. This place is too hard for me." Impatiently I reply, "Well listen, you're gonna have to make up your mind." Duran inquires, "What do you get for an awol?" Author, "I don't know, I don't know what your staff's gonna give you; but I do know that you're gonna have to go to bed. Your staff (refer-

ring to his social worker) is not here, so you have one of two choices—
either to go to bed or awol. Duran then acknowledges Willis by saying,
"Well let me talk to 'Willis' for a while." Thus Shorty and I leave the
room, permitting Willis and Duran a private session. Shorty and I simply
stand outside of room seven talking as other night staff joined us.

Anxious about Duran's decision, I re-entered the room, saying, "O.K.,
what are you gonna do? Are you gonna stay or go." Duran, "I'm gonna
stay." Author, "O.K. then hurry up and wrap this up 'cause you can't stay
up this late." Here, it is a weeknight and currently 10:30pm; residents are
due in bed at 9pm. Not only has my shift ended and I'm ready to go home
but it is important that the Home be stable before I leave, given my
position. If problems occur during my shift, I am required to stay and assist
until problems or crises are resolved. It follows that Willis and Duran
rapidly completed their session, Duran went to bed, Willis completed an
incident report and I went Home.

The Mata Case

The next instance illustrates intelligence on the resident's part, e.g., his
tactical plan to escape, and a lack of knowledge (regarding the structure of
San Bernarndino Juvenile Hall, S.B.J.H.) on the part of staff. Clearly the
resident is at an advantage, for he is from San Bernarndino and was
recruited from S.B.J.H. and placed at Opportunity Boys' Home. It also
suggest that these particular staff had no intention of retrieving a stray resident (Mata), working within the legitimate confines of their job. The
actions by Raymond and Ricardo illustrate that they will do no more or less
for the institution, not to mention staff ultimately construct awol reports.

After several violations, Z-dorm staff decided to terminate Mata
because he was (again) caught smoking marijuana. Raymond and Ricardo
were to transport him to juvenile hall yet both were concerned about Mata
awoling during the fifty-five mile trip. While they drove, Raymond notes,
"Mata was talking about turning himself in and that when he arrived at
San Bernarndino Juvenile Hall, he (Mata) was going to take a shower and
go to bed." Raymond and Ricardo felt that Mata was conning them; thus
according to Raymond, he and Ricardo looked at one another wondering,
"does he really think we believe that?" Moreover, during the trip,
Raymond and Ricardo were concerned about when and how Mata would
make his great escape. Raymond figured that "Mata would run at a stop
light, but he did not. Mata waited until we drove up into the drive way of

San Bernarndino Juvenile Hall, then opened the van door and ran off."
Raymond and Ricardo observed from the front seats of the van as Mata
escaped in to the streets.

Neither staff ran after Mata, nor did they appear disturbed by his awol.
They appeared somewhat indifferent and began explaining the structure of
S.B.J.H. According to Raymond, S.B.J.H. does not have automatic security
gates that open and close for vehicles when inmates arrive (as does Central
Juvenile Hall in Los Angeles). One simply parks and walks the inmate to
the detention area. I sensed Raymond placing blame on the structure of
S.B.J.H., which makes awoling possible. They simply reported the awol to
S.B.J.H. officials and submitted an awol report to OBH. Now, Mata's
probation officer is responsible for locating him and placing him (Mata) in
juvenile hall.

The Brown Case

Finally, how do OBH staff respond to a physically threatening resident?
And, what tactics are used by Brown (resident) in an attempt to reverse his
terminal condition? This awol shows certain stall tactics, albeit eventually,
staff grew tired of the resident's delay tactics and excuses. Moreover, staff's
attempt to counsel and reason with this resident became exhausting and
fruitless, resulting in staff urging and encouraging his swift departure.
Consider the following awol:

While working in the O.D. office, I (O.D.) received a call from Mara
(Y-dorm counselor), exclaiming that Brown (Y-dorm resident) had
physically threatened her. Mara demanded that Brown be removed from
dorm-Y and taken to juvenile hall. Arriving in Y-dorm, Mara immediately
insisted, "Brown has to go! He cannot be down here threatening staff, and
staff is not gonna feel intimidated by him!!"

Brown had left the dorm and was on the playing field talking with
Dick Fox (Y-dorm counselor). Down on the field, I observed Dick and
Brown talking. Dick ventured to mediate between Mara and Brown.
Brown was explaining and reviewing his interpretation of the incident,
while Dick not only reinterpreted Brown's view but sought to advise and
counsel Brown.

The encounter between Dick and Brown was very emotional as each
tried to convince the other by acting out their versions. For example,
Brown would back away from Dick, then move forward, pointing towards
the dorm, pleading, "I didn't wanna have anything to do with Mara, I just

wanted her to leave me alone. I wasn't gonna say nothing to nobody."
Dick: "It would have been nice if you'd of said it that way, but you stood up
and shouted (now Dick is imitating Brown's previous movements) 'don't
tell me what to do, just leave me the fuck alone!!'" This sort of
conversation went on for nearly five to seven minutes before the O.D. intervened. At one point Dick charged, "Brown we're always on you about
somethin'. We're tellin' you--pull your pants up, you're saggin', or take
the comb out of your hair or change your clothes because you got the
wrong colors on. If you just followed the rules, no one would bother you.
But somehow, you think you're running things around here." Brown:
"That's what I was gonna do. I was gonna do my room time, and I wasn't
gonna fuck with nobody. Because, you know, when you dealin' with these
staff, I'm always gonna lose, you know I can't win, so why not follow the
rules." Dick: "Right!" Brown: "And that's just what I was gonna do."
Dick: "But you haven't been doing it." Observing the encounter, Brown
had an answer and justification for all Dick's questions.

After feeling that they were going in circles, I intervened, giving
Brown the "bottom line," "Look, the decision has been made, Mara wants
you in juvenile hall. Now either you can go to juvenile hall or awol?"
Brown: "I shouldn't have to go to the hall!!" Author, "You've been
conferenced about this all day. You were conferenced by Inga..." Brown
interrupts, "I didn't talk to Inga!!" Author, "Well I talked to Inga and quite
frankly, we're sick of your shit. Now you can either go to the hall or awol,
but you can't stay here!"

Now consider Mara's version of the incident:

"Well we were in group and there was a resident, I think it was Larson,
sitting between me and Brown. I reminded Brown about what his P.O. and
Inga said about juvenile hall. He got mad and started threatening staff
again: 'I'm not goin' to the hall for just touching somebody!' He (Brown)
demonstrated this by tapping Larson on the arm. He (Brown) laughed and
looked at me and said, 'I'm tellin' you staff gonna make me go off!!' Then
Brown moved to the end of the seat, looked at me and swung his arm
around like he was gonna hit me. I just sat there. I didn't move. (Mara
pauses, then begins to laugh as she continues). I thought I was a 'goner'.
Now to really be honest, I felt chills goin' up and down my spine. Then I
asked him to leave the room but he didn't. He just went to the door and
stood up, and started swaying from side to side. There Brown continued to
make threats about how he would 'hurt somebody' if he had to go to the

hall." Author, "And this is when you called me?" Mara, "Well, it was shortly after."

Brown then walks towards the dorm. I trail him (Brown) and Dick brings up the rear. Brown goes straight to his room to pack while I stand outside his room observing and Dick enters Brown's room, attempting to further reason with him. That is, Dick advised Brown to go to the hall so that the probability of Brown returning was higher. Brown argued, "I am no fool, I'm not going to the hall because they ain't gonna bring me back!!" Dick: "How do you know that?" Brown: "You know why I say that?" Dick: "Why?" Brown: "Because there is only two people who can let be come back here. Ms. Ballen and Inga, and Inga don't like me. And another reason, because of my size (Brown is six feet and muscular). If Antonio (smaller Y-dorm resident) would've done what I did, nothin' would've happened to him. But it's because of my size. These staff feel threatened by me." Dick: "No we're not threatened by you." Brown: "Well intimidated."
Brown felt that Dick could not understand his decision to awol for Dick was not "in my shoes". Brown reasoned, "See man, know why you say that? 'Cause you not in my shoes. If you was in my shoes you'd awol too!! Let me go ask Mara!!" Then Brown walks out of his room, down the hall into the dorm office. Mara is seated behind the desk, writing an incident report. By now, more staff arrived to monitor the situation. Dick, Eduardo, Claude and myself closely trail Brown into the office. Then Brown asked, "Mara, if I don't mess up no more tonight, do I still have to go to the hall?" Mara, "This is like a cooling off period. If you go and do good, you might be able to come back." Brown, "But I didn't hit you?" Mara, "Brown, we been over that already. Your P.O. was here today and Inga made a special trip up here. She said any intimidation, threats or physicals you'd be going to the hall..." O.D. interrupts addressing Brown, "I've been listenin' to you talk to Dick, Claude and Mara. And you know, you don't listen to anyone, you have an answer or excuse for everything. Look, the fact of the matter is, you don't want to awol... Brown interrupts, "I don't?!" I continue, "...you want to go to the hall but you're scare of what your friends will say!!" Brown shrugs his shoulders as if to say "that's not true." The O.D. proceeds, "But the fact of the matter is, you're either goin' to the hall or leaving, but you need to stop this stalling." Brown then leaves the office, walking towards his room to pack slowly and carefully.
As Brown packed, two Y-dorm counselors (Dick & Claude, at various times, sometimes simultaneously) attempted to persuade Brown to chose

"the hall." This too may have contributed to Brown's hesitant awol. Observing this scene, I actually watched Brown pack very slowly; he folded every garment (that he owned) neatly and placed it in his brown leather baggage. He packed so carefully that all his clothing fit, and when he experienced trouble with a large pair of Levi Jeans, Brown removed the jeans from his bag, re-folded and re-packed. Inside his room, Brown talked with counselors and packed, while Eduardo and I stood outside of his open door observing. Brown took such a long time that on occasion, Eduardo and I would wander the dorm, walking the hallway, and going in and out of the office. Brown spent nearly 45 minutes packing.

At one point, Dick resigned his attempts to persuade Brown and left the room. Dick went to the water fountain (next to Y-dorm entrance door and office), and while Brown was in his room alone, I mentioned to Dick, "You wanna be sure that he doesn't take someone else's clothes." Brown heard my comment, thus rushed out of his room and immediately defended himself from my apparent insinuation. Holding his clothes up, Brown declared, "These are my clothes and I'm not stealing no body else's!!" I sternly stared at Brown as he went back to his room.

When Brown finally finished, he did as one does when checking out of a hotel. That is, he made a final check, making certain not to leave anything. He moved his bed, looking over, around and under it. He reexamined his closet, leaving empty bottles of shampoo and other articles (papers, pencils, hangers) on the top closet shelf. Then, he checked his dresser draws, opening and closing them, but taking nothing out.

There were Y-dorm residents hovering about Brown's room, in the hallway and entrance door. As Brown was leaving their attention became glued to him. Brown was even shocked by all the attention, smiling and remarking, "Is this an audience?" Brown shook hands with two of his peers, saying aloud so everyone could hear, "I'm gone, I'll check you later, I'll call you when get home." Then Brown went for a final drink of water (from the water fountain) and left.

After Brown completely left Y-dorm and proceeded off grounds the O.D. walked inside of Y-dorm, and seeing both residents and staff, I asked Mara to come to the O.D. office so she could privately convey her full story. However, before she began, I noticed Brown being detained. Gazing from the O.D. office window, Allen (W-dorm coordinator, who lives on grounds yet was off duty) was driving off campus but stopped to speak with Brown. A short while later, Allen had pulled his car in front of Y-dorm and Brown was waiting (by the flag pole) talking with Ben (W-dorm counselor). I was bewildered and walked down to meet Allen as he proceeded up the stairs towards W-dorm. When we (Allen & O.D.) met, Allen was at the bottom of the stairs and I was on the top. In a baffled way, I inquired, "What's goin' on Allen?" Allen, "Brown says he burned his breeches in Y-dorm and he was gonna awol. But I told him that he could stay in my dorm until Monday, then maybe they could straighten it out." O.D., "No!! He cannot stay in W-dorm. Brown knows his situation. He can either go to the hall or leave. This whole thing has been cleared through Inga and Y-dorm. So you need to tell him that he can't stay in your dorm." After demanding that Allen reverse his suggestion, I sensed that Allen felt that he had made a big mistake. That is, Allen gestured in a manner that indicated he interfered and needed to clean up his mistake (Allen's face dropped).

Allen then calls out for Brown who stood in the flagpole circle conversing with Ben. Allen yelled, "Brown, Brown!" Apparently, Brown did not hear him, so he called again, "Brown, Brown!" Brown looks over. Allen, "Come here." Brown walks partially towards Allen and myself, then Allen explains, "Brown, you can't stay here, you gotta go to the hall. So you might as well let your staff take you to the hall so that way you might be back in a week or two." Allen's car door was left open when he got out, and after Allen advised Brown, Allen slowly drifts towards his car. Then Brown concludes, "See, I told you they wasn't gonna let me stay." Allen, "Why don't you go to the hall and make it easier on yourself. See the only reason I'm tellin' you this is because I live here and I've seen too many guys make the wrong decision." Brown, "Man, I'm not goin' to the hall! They ain't gonna let me come back here!" Allen, "Am I wastin' my time?" Brown, "They ain't gonna bring me back!" Allen, "Am I wastin' my time?" Brown delivers a very submissive, "No, but I'm not going to the hall." Allen gets into his car and drives off; Brown proceeds to walk out of the gates. Walking with a huge and seemingly heavy brown leather bag over his shoulder, Brown reaches the entrance/exit area and appears indecisive. That is, watching him from a distance, Brown steps right then left and continues left; probably up to the corner to catch the bus.

In this case, juvenile hall was out of the question for Brown; he believed that OBH officials would never reconsider him. Of his two choices, Brown elected to awol. Though he awoled, it is debatable whether he really wanted to depart, for at every turn, Brown was trying to rectify his situation to remain at OBH. Seemingly, he wanted to say but this option was not available. While staff became exhausted, they advised and recommended juvenile hall. "The hall" is a step down from placement, yet the possibility of returning clearly exist. Moreover, "the hall" is the official line of recommendation from staff to residents in this situation. That is, the institution is willing to transport residents to the hall, but unwilling to utilize institutional vehicles for awoling. Again, awoling clearly violates one's court ordered placement. Staff used these options ("the hall" or awoling) to maintain control. In the final analysis, Brown could not stay; he had to leave.

In every case, there is a distinct awol process which staff and residents experience. Some awols are planned, others are spontaneous yet in every case, there appears an implicit or explicit message that is interpreted by staff (received from awolees). In the first scenario, Duran not only wanted attention and desired to display and make others aware of his ability to construct a dummy. He was proud of his "art" and wanted to "get away" undetected. Mata's awol seems to convey that he was tired of L.A. and simply needed a ride back to San Bernardino. Presumably, Brown was crying for help, but did not know how to accepted it, until it was too late. He desired to maintain a certain image (of himself) to fellow residents, e.g., he was in charge of himself, other residents and dominant over staff. The issue is control, and how staff use awoling and juvenile hall to maintain authority. If residents are unwilling to cooperate, then awoling is an option. Leaving rids staff of this particular problem and the object of trouble disappears.

Awol Returns

How does the "return process" humble residents? When residents return from awol, they are not likely to act-out but appear very humble and cooperative. The "return process" involves five stages that include **searching, questioning, instruction, counseling** and **sanctioning**. Documentation is also part of this process in that staff are required to record Y-resident's return and his mental condition (in the main and dorm logs).

Procedurally, when residents return from awol (by relatives, by friends, by bus or walking) they are required to report the O.D. office. Here the resident is typically searched and questioned by the O.D. The purpose of **searching** is to prevent contraband from entering the institution. If contraband is found, the O.D. is likely to confiscate any item in question. The

O.D. then documents the resident's return, informs his dorm staff and instructs the resident to return to his dorm. The O.D. also erases the individual's name from the "felt board," which lists all awol residents. If the individual's name remains under the awol heading, OBH is required to accept such returning awolees. Primarily because Y-resident is still being counted as part of the overall OBH residential population, thereby OBH continues to receive payment for such residents. There is another column that list all resident terminations. If, for example, Y-resident was listed under the awol column, then after ten days moved to the termination column, OBH is not required to accept such residents. In this situation, the O.D. will inform the resident of his termination, instruct him to return home and call his probation officer.

Though this procedure of going directly to the O.D. office is formalized, it does not necessarily work as planned. That is, residents may not initially report to the O.D. office; but a resident may decide to report to his dorm staff, or go to his dorm room, or to the gym and even to another dorm to inform a friend of his return. This gets at the openness of the facility, and their (residents) ability to sneak in (smuggle) contraband without much effort or hassle from staff.

In practice and on occasion, the searching procedure seems equally lax. That is, some residents are not searched; on other occasions, the O.D. may "pass the buck" to dorm staff, instructing them to search; still other residents are permitted to search themselves. For example, the O.D. or staff might not be fully cognizant of residents searching themselves. Staff may request that returning residents take off their jackets, shoes and socks, uncuff their pants, and empty the contents within their pockets onto the desk. Meanwhile the staff may be busy talking on the phone and haphazardly examining the contents.

Dorm counselors and O.D.s are not required to "feel search" the resident's body as police search criminals. Staff however are required to examine the content of the resident's articles. That is, to look through the resident's wallet, take his jacket and thoroughly inspect pockets and lining, and search inside of his shoes. If for example, a resident returns with a radio, tape recorder, bag of clothes and a shoebox of his personal belongings, staff are required to thoroughly search all such articles. There are times when strip searches are recommended. That is, a female staff may ask a male staff to strip search a resident who she believes is concealing contraband. In such a case, a male staff takes the resident into a private restroom, instructing him to remove all clothing or simply "drop your pants and underwear." While the resident reveals his private parts, staff then inspects the anal, gentile and armpit areas. Residents who refuse strip searches are placed "on hold" until the staff's suspicion is resolved.

During the process of searching, staff commonly question residents and give them instructions. Typical **questions** are: "why did you leave?" "Why'd you come back?" "Do you plan to change your behavior?" "What'd you bring back?" "How'd you get back?" "How long do you plan to stay *this time?*" "Where'd you go?" and "What'd you do while awoled?" Questions are asked to receive a sense of the resident's disposition. It gives staff a chance to eyeball residents (to see if their eyes are reddish and glazed) and resident responses permit staff to smell any type of substance. Intoxication of returnees is a major concern for staff, so they (staff) are aware of the resident's condition and his possible effect on others. **Instructions** are issued to remind the resident that he has returned to placement thereby expected to behave appropriately. Consider Raymond's questions and instructions:

> When we entered V-Dorm, Raymond was standing and I informed him that Acuna (resident) had returned from awol and had not been searched. Raymond simply took over, as he asked and stood ready to search Acuna: "Did you do any drugs? Did you bring anything back with you?" Acuna does not verbally answer, he simply nods his head in a no motion. Then Raymond asked Acuna to empty his pockets and place the contents on the desk. Acuna did not place the contents on the desk but actually placed the contents in Raymond's hand. Acuna handed Raymond a cassette tape, it was white with gang writing on the both sides. Raymond commented, "I'm gonna confiscate this tape because it has gang writing on it." Raymond throws the tape near Maggie (on the desk). Acuna does not respond and Raymond continues to search. Raymond then addresses Acuna, "These guys are up for all kinds of war stories, like how much dope you smoked, how good the sherm was, and how many women you screwed. But I don't want you to spread these stories, O.K.?!" Acuna nods his head in a yes motion as Raymond continues to search.

Staff recognize that residents are at a disadvantage when they return; residents appear more humble and willing to follow instructions and counsel. This humbleness, in part, appears as a consequence of the resident's ignorance concerning his destiny at OBH and anxiety about sanctions. Turning themselves in signals a kind of surrender, e.g., "I'll do anything to stay." When **counseled** about their return, responses range from confessions to excuses to last resorts. For instance, Portillo claims that he returned because "they were going to fill my bed space." Reed alleged that his godfather insisted on his return. Morrison rationalized that "I couldn't get in touch with my girlfriend." Maldanodo confessed that "I found out that they were not gonna terminate me." And Trujillo reasoned that "I want to try it again. You know, I'm gonna give it two months. If I'm not doing a good program I'll probably leave." Counselors receive other rationales about awol returns, however staff's function during this stage is to understand the resident's awol reason, suggest ways to prevent future awols and inform the resident as to where he stands at OBH.

Most residents who return have in fact avoided the most damaging sanction, i.e., termination. But it is also clear that the **sanctions** residents do receive upon return are quite bearable. That is, it is quite common for residents to receive a "status drop", lose privileges for two weeks, and the elimination of home visits (home passes) for six weeks. Informing residents of sanctions usually comes at the close of the counseling session. All such "consequences" are designed to keep residents close to Home. Moreover, all such "consequences" are negotiable over time. That is, residents may obtain privileges before two weeks and home visits may resume prior to six weeks. All of which depends on the type of awol, the resident's behavior, and staff's re-evaluation of residents. If however, residents' awol and return to frequently, it is quite probable to anticipate a termination. But for the most part, residents are searched, questioned, instructed, counseled and informed of their penalty.

Notes

1. Successfully complete the program.

2. Generally speaking, awols address the boarder theoretical issue of escapes. When residents' awol, they are escaping from authority (or semi-confinement) to some type of independence (or freedom). While incarcerated criminals, prisoners of wars, and inmates in Nazi concentration camps are "totally confined," they too generally escaped for similar reasons. Historically, several African Americans are among this group who sought freedom from a cruel caste system, slavery.

    Escaping from total institutions often requires tactical planning. In the case of Captain Lulu Lawton, who escaped from Germany's POW Colditz

Castle during World War II, he watched for months the comings and goings of visitors to and from the Castle. He discovered that a small group of Polish POWs arrived with two German military escorts three times weekly, at approximately 7am, carrying boxes, leaving after a half hour, with a shift change of German officers also occurring at 7am (Cavendish, 1983). After enlisting three others, they eventually devised a scheme to march out of the impregnable Castle through the main gate.

Other escapes are equally suspenseful, as when Bill Harris made an all-night swim through shark-infested waters from Corregidor to Bataan, managing to escape a Corregidor POW prison camp (Whitcomb, 1958); and when Henry "Box" Brown escaped slavery by mailing himself to freedom in Philadelphia (Bennett, 1964). Audiences are awed by magicians who free themselves from tight straps, locked cases and underwater enclosures. Likewise the people of Virginia and prison administration were frightfully amazed when the Mecklenburg Six escaped from the Mecklenburg Correctional Center. They constructed an ingenious plan that "took absolute control of the Death Row area, posed as prison guards, ordered a van, directed the gates to be opened, and drove away from the penitentiary, issuing one final command, 'Close the gates!'" (Dance, 1987). Magicians as well as prisoners are attempting to outsmart their audience and/or gatekeepers, respectively. The idea, whether resident, slave, magician, criminal, POW, or inmate in concentration camp is to free oneself from an unpleasant condition. Often the condition is one of alienation, self-estrangement, and force causing victims to seek and achieve some type of release. Typically, the plan and consequences are considered prior to escape; thus each individual who becomes a fugitive is quite likely to be aware of the punishment, and if caught, willing to accept whatever sanctions applied.

3. It should be noted that in rare cases, staff are unable to construct awol explanations, thereby writing "unknown" in the space provided.

4. Also see Hammersley and Atkinson (*Ethnography Principles in Practice*, 1983) for developing typologies.

5. The Brown case is discussed in the next section, "the process of awoling."

6. When Morrison returned from his first awol, it was not during my shift. Presumably, he was cooperative for the morning O.D. during the search.

7. This conversation occurred on December 15th, 1987.

Chapter 7

Resident Leaving: Juvenile Hall

Juvenile hall is considered the worst and most severe sanction applied to residents. It is a last resort response to maintaining control and restoring order. "The hall" signifies placement failure; it is a type of downward mobility that transfers one from an open facility to a locked-down total institution. Placement demotion (going to the hall) suggests that residents are unable to adjust to their new-open environment and in need of placement in a more restrictive setting.

In juvenile hall, for example, rooms, units and/or cells are often locked; the entire institution is fenced in, surveillance is tighter, privacy is limited, and uniforms are common. Guards are not interested in treatment but obedience and confinement. Their attitudes towards inmates are impersonal and detached, while physical restraint is a very real and frequent option for staff. At times, the confinement atmosphere is one of fear and distrust; consequently, dangerous conflicts (fights, stabbing, and even deaths) between guard and inmates or inmates and inmates are likely to occur in juvenile hall. Inmates who engage in dangerous conflicts are frequently "boxed", where they are isolated from the hall community.

Conversely, placement requires no "uniforms," residents receive home and community passes, dorm rooms remain unlock, and while the facility is enclosed, the front entrance consistently remains open. Most residents prefer placement to juvenile hall, for there are far more "freedoms" and fewer constraints. Part of ones attraction to placement are the amenities, e.g., home passes, store passes, field trips, interaction with female residents (from other placements), the freedom to own and play radios, the ability earn money, and "eggs to order" Monday through Friday (during break-fast). Indeed, the general function of treatment institutions (placements) is to provide opportunities for residents to rehabilitate themselves, returning to mainstream society.

Juvenile hall and placement denotes the difference between total institutions and semi-total institutions, respectively. Semi total institutions are dissimilar from Goffman's (*Asylums*, 1964:4) description of total institutions. Semi-total institutions refer to settings that are not entirely closed and separated from the outside world; physical restraints and boundaries are not necessarily present. Here, boundaries and restraints are more psychological. There are however some very key similarities, e.g., rigid rules, involuntary admittance, informal rules, standard food and ac-tivities, and manipulation by staff.

Before any resident is sent to juvenile hall, he is "cleared" by his probation officer and "the hall" itself. Clearance then involves calling the probation officer to inform him that OBH has decided to terminate his client. In turn, the probation officer calls juvenile hall officials informing them that his client has been terminated and will be returning to juvenile hall. OBH also contacts "the hall" making certain that probation officers have in fact appraised "hall" officials of the situation, and making sure that there is sufficient space for an additional inmate. If proper clearance is not attained or there is insufficient hall space, juvenile hall officials have been known to refuse placement residents. OBH is required to retain resident until hall space becomes available.

Threats, Evaluations and Contracts as Punishment

As discussed earlier, basic, significant and collective sanctions are used to address resident infractions and potentially modify behavior. These sanctions contain a deprivation/restrictive quality. However, threats, evaluations and contracts are used by staff as alternative methods to basic and significant punishments. "Alternative methods" involve a longer-term response to resident violations than basic and significant sanctions, especially contracts, which involve fundamental changes in the resident's life situation. Residents who enter the "alternative" cycle are often ex-periencing chronic misconduct, frustrating staff because "nothing has worked." Staff then find it necessary to crack down by using "hall" threats, formal/informal evaluations and contracts.

Generally, there is a kind of resistance by residents to return to juvenile hall when faced with termination. The thought of losing privileges and "freedoms" often fuels resistance. In the previous chapter, I examine how some residents awol instead of return to "the hall."[1] Staff belief, nevertheless, that the threat of social demotion (juvenile hall) seems to provide a certain socio-psychological and physical control over residents. More often than not, when staff threaten residents with juvenile hall (during group or private conferences) various residents modify their actions, often contemplating a situation that one does not wish to relive. Charles (X-dorm resident) recalled that he was threatened with juvenile hall by Rob Bans (X-dorm social worker) and thought, "I don't want to go back to the hall, that place is crazy." At some point then (through awoling instead of returning to the hall, hearing resident talk about the hall, and by residents modifying their behavior based on "hall" threats), staff learn that residents really dislike and resent returning to juvenile hall. Actual terminations however function as behavioral incentives for entire dorms; they are general deterrence (Henshel, 1990) for other residents. Eventually, staff learn to manipulate the threat of juvenile hall to their advantage, e.g., marshalling a type of control and therefore formal power to establish residential conformity.

Not only do staff threats and actual terminations impact residents, but staff formal and informal evaluations influence residential behavior. Ulti-mately, it is line staff who work with residents, having the most social contact, and thereby being in position to construct judgments on their behavior, e.g., their progress or lack thereof. Being able to form evaluations of residents now places staff in a position to make recommendations. Recommendations may range from selecting residents to attend a movie screening, to resident termination, to further residential treatment. It follows that most residents recognize that staff have authority to shape and effect their institutional life experience through evaluations.

Before residents are formally told and taken to "the hall," there are often informal hints and remarks by staff. That is, staff may become so aggravated by certain ongoing rule violations, e.g., fights, awols, gang attire, and school problems that they casually suggest to residents that they might return to the hall if their behavior does not improve. During group or individual counseling sessions staff have frequently communicated to certain "border line" residents, that "I spoke to your P.O. (probation officer) today and he said one more fuck up and you're on your way to the hall." In short, residents receive some sense that their behavior is inappropriate which could result in termination (juvenile hall). But the extent to which residents take staff warning seriously is debatable.[2] That is, inmate behavior appears temporarily effected.

In the case of Marcus (social worker), those residents who are on the brink of termination are asked to sign a "contract." That is, an individual counseling session is scheduled and conducted in which residents are given a documented history of their behavior and informed of the contract conditions. Residents are more or less forced to sign the agreement, and failure to abide by the agreement terminates problem residents from OBH. Essentially, the contract mandates that residents have "two weeks to straighten up or ship out."

Given the coercive nature of contracts, residents take caution, for resisting could terminate their placement. Most residents recognize that contracts are essentially "second chances." Many residents who do not receive this option often request being placed on contract; in short, they are asking for another chance, "a warning," according to Kiman (staff). While "telling residents" often has its behavioral advantages, one major disadvantage is staff failure to enforce the contract. When contracts are not enforced, due to low residential population, agreements lose value, permitting residents to manipulate and think lit of contracts.

Marcus flatly disagrees with contracts because administrators and social workers do not take them seriously. One problem with contracts is that "they don't follow up with it. If you use it, you gotta follow up with it. The kids read it like a joke and kids know the game...So when it (JH) happens, its a shock." Marcus reasons that contracts have little effect over residential behavior in that some residents supply very lucrative monetary offerings to the economy of OBH:

> The kind of money they get for these kids, they're not gonna get rid of them; it comes down to money. They (administrators) really don't have to deal with the kids. Unless he does something really severe, those administrators gonna do everything they can to keep him here.

Administrators have blocked contractual terminations. Such intervention results from low residential population, which could translate into financial hardship for the institution. Residents bring-in $2800 per month, yet if they are terminated, OBH is not paid. Staff believes that administrative concerns are often economic, and such a position is often inconsistent and conflictual with treatment philosophies. When this happens, staff's morale seems lowered, citing the contradictions of contracts and administrative unwillingness to support the treatment wishes (or really control methods) of line-staff. Administrators may very well view the institution as a business first, and treatment facility second. Though line staff view OBH in the opposite direction. And since "they" (administrators) not only have power, and "really don't have to deal with the kids," "they" make decisions that effect the overall quality of the institution.

Residents, however, who do not receive contracts go straight to juvenile hall and usually told that they may return to Opportunity Home if their attitude and behavior in juvenile hall improves. Generally, such residents are viewed as threats to the institutional structure of OBH. According to Kiman, "some staff are intimidated by residents; they don't want to be bothered with them. A big kid who intimidates is gone; he won't have as many chances as a smaller resident." Similarly, Marcus argues that residents who don't receive contracts are viewed by therapists and administrators as "threats to the place". Marcus described a situation concerning a "kid who set a fire in front of X-dorm. Once Nash (Executive Director) heard about it, he didn't get a contract, he was just gone!"

In large measure, obtaining contracts appear to have behavioral conditions attached. Those residents who are "threats to the place" are not likely to receive contracts. Shari conceded that "contracts weren't needed in every case; it depended on the incident and situation." More importantly, abrupt behavioral terminations signals to staff and residents what is absolutely prohibited (setting fires), revealing the authority of those who can marshal instantaneous terminations. Certain staff may feel they have been grossly violated by residents but lack power to enforce their recommended termination. So staff and residents learn to revere those (executive & clinical directors, intake worker) who have demonstrated an ability to terminate residents and staff.

Precipitating Incidents

There are various precipitating factors that lead to ones return to juvenile hall. Some factors are more serious than others. That is, some precipitating incidents continually gnaw at staff patience, giving them no other option; conversely, other singular incidents might be so serious that staff simply react, insisting on the resident's immediate return to juvenile hall.

In the first case, where precipitating incidents continually gnaw at staff patience, residents are often involved in **minor** run-ins and mess-ups that lead to the loss of staff support, thus a recommendation of juvenile hall. Residents who continually abuse OBH openness by awoling home, to the store and/or to Taco Bell (fast food restaurant) are often targeted towards juvenile hall. The same is true for residents who continually fight, steal or "run their own program." The real issue here is the process by which these persistent **minor** infractions are handled. That is, what remedies are used to correct inappropriate behaviors? The process begins with "warnings". "Warnings" include, but are not limited to, counseling, documenting behavior in incident reports and logs, and issuing sanctions. Then, staff progressively moves to "contracts," and if contracts are not adhered to, staff recommend the final stage, "action." That is, a return to juvenile hall.

Michela's incident report is a case in point for tracking continual **minor** offenses leading to a loss of staff support. She writes:

> Eric cursed-out staff after being denied a pass to the gym. Earlier in the evening, Eric approached Jen (social worker) in a very hostile and threatening manner. Eric has a pattern of hostility and intimidation towards most of the staff. I am concerned about these re-occurring incidents of threatening through glaring looks of hostility and verbal abusiveness and confrontations. It appears that each cycle he chooses a different staff. He appears more aggressive each time.

Here, Michela clearly documents her "concern about these re-occurring incidents." The extent to which Michela is frustrated and "burnt-out" with Eric is very real, so real that she issues specific attention getting sanctions. That is, Michela placed Eric on hold, gave him a room restriction and convened a conference with herself, Eric and Janette Ballen (administrator). What is the function of this conference? Such conferences are designed to "read residents the riot act!!" That is, straighten up or be terminated to juvenile hall.

Serious violations are also considered precipitating factors that lead to juvenile hall. The process is not as extensive, in fact, it is very much abbreviated. **Serious** violations, such as fires and residents who are considered "threats to the place," receive immediate *action*, e.g., an immediate return to juvenile hall. For instance, after Brown (resident) verbally threatened Mara (counselor), staff was left with one alternative, juvenile hall. Moreover, Marcus (staff) cites a case where a "kid who set a fire in front of X-dorm" was terminated after Nash (executive director) "heard about it." And finally, after Nash's daughter was frightened by Glen (resident), he too was terminated. Consider the entire incident:

Before and during dinner, there was a y-dorm resident (Glen) who was OGA (on grounds awol) and running his own program. Glen ran all over campus but especially the hill, which is directly behind X-Dorm, Y-dorm and Z-dorm. One portion of the hill is not developed; there are many weeds, bushes, trees, a chicken coop (near the top), old car tires, old water hoses, etc. The other portion is developed, containing OBH chapel and three feet way (from the Chapel) is Nash's home. His house is owned by OBH. While looking down from the hill, near the Chapel or Nash's house, one has a good view of the facility. When Glen initially awoled, Jen and Rhee (Y-dorm social workers) physically escorted him (Glen) to the O.D. office and ordered him to "sit down!!" Glen wiggled his way out of their hold, insisting: "I don't have to stay here!!" Then Glen got up, walked out of the O.D. office and front lobby, proceeded down the stairs, awoling through the front gate. In the darkened evening, Rhee and Jen watched as Glen exited the gate.

Then Glen would return to literally play "hide and seek" with staff. During dinner, Nash informed me that his daughter called complaining that there was a resident on the hill, near Nash's house-window. In his P.R. way, Nash smiled and instead of asking, he said: "Paul'll go check it out." So with a sigh I said, "Yeah, I'll check it out." (Note: Nash's daughter is thirty years).

While searching on this dark hill, three other staff joined me: Claude, Craig (new employee) and Rhee. We did not spot him initially; but as we broke up and acquired flashlights (from Nash's house), we eventually spotted Glen. Glen is a small-thin Black resident from San Bernandino County. Craig was first to meet up with him, though Glen was outside of the hill gate (on the other side of Nash's house; in short, Glen was off OBH property. Glen carried a bamboo stick, as he ran from us, exclaiming "the party's about to begin!!" But soon Glen evaded us—that is, Rhee and myself remained on the hill calling out for Craig and/or Glen but there was no reply; so we eventually left the hill.

After returning and settling in the kitchen for five minutes, the panic button rang. The O.D. panel indicated X-dorm so many staff rushed to X-dorm, discovering that Glen had gone out the back way and back up the dark hill. This time more staff ran up the hill, including Nash, Jen & Marie (there were about three more staff). On the hill, we met Nash's daughter in their back patio area. She seemed nervous and afraid; she was also out of breath from her running and apparent anxiety. She told us that she was in the garage and that someone (probably Glen) turned off the lights. At that point, other staff were coming up the hill and I instructed them to return for we had enough staff already. Nash commented that "this is the first time that this has ever happened." But he too appeared nervous and avowed to "stay here" with his daughter; in Nash's word's "I'm gonna stay up here." I thought to myself, "good!"

Then we dispersed again searching for Glen on the hill; We went further up the hill, near the chicken coop; thus slipping and sliding on the hill, in the bushes, not knowing what might be up there (or in there); any type of animal (skunk) could have appeared. But on the hill, Glen consistently eluded us; we threw rocks in bushes where he might hide; Nash, his daughter, and Jen, stood on a lower portion of the hill (near the chapel) as we searched. We searched and searched, becoming very frustrated that Glen could eluded us and this one resident was causing so much commotion. The search party consisted of Craig, Claude, Rhee, myself, Trib. Mara and Evia were standing at the bottom of the hill, behind Y-dorm and they spotted Glen going up the side of the hill; they yelled out: "there he is, there he is!!!" We rushed to the general area in which they were pointing. We ran down to retrieve Glen as he ran further up the hill trying to free himself. But Craig caught and restrained (choked) him. Claude and myself assisted Craig yet as Glen stopped wiggling, I loosened my grip and let Claude and Craig hold Glen.

We walked down the hill holding Glen; as we passed Nash, his daughter and Jen, I asked Nash: "Do you want us to take him to juvenile hall?" Nash supplied a timid, "Yes." Thus, I instructed Craig and Claude to take Glen directly to the van. In the meantime, I obtained the van keys from the O.D. cabinet.

For Nash, this incident was serious because Glen frightened Nash's daughter and temporarily eluded many OBH staff. Glen's attention getting awol, his ability to allude authority and comment regarding "I don't have to stay here," may have suggested to Nash that open placement is not appropriate for Glen. That is, the extent to which Glen could be controlled may have been doubtful to Nash. Moreover, Glen created an environment that was unsafe for Nash's daughter, and most fathers desire to protect their children from danger. Thus Glen was sentenced to the most severe sanction, juvenile hall.

The real difference between **minor** violations versus **serious** violations as precipitating factors is response time. On the one hand, a resident's time is extended so that staff might exhaust all *first resort* remedies. While on the other, there is little or no talk of options, believing that there is only one solution, e.g. juvenile hall.

Juvenile Hall: Telling Residents

How staff inform residents of their termination and return to juvenile hall may pose serious dilemmas. Some staff prefer to openly tell residents while others chose deception. The danger of openly *telling residents* is that they may awol, and/or act-out in the process of *telling*. The advantage of "telling residents" is that staff could saved a trip to juvenile hall (were the resident to awol); and/or the resident could actually go peacefully, thus affording him an opportunity to return to OBH.

Those staff who oppose *telling residents* argue that it creates an "unnecessary scene" (possible fight between "terminatee" and a resident who may have assisted staff by giving them information on the terminatee), possible conflicts between staff and "terminatee", "terminatee" may awol, and/or "terminatee" could steal from other residents. Don Benton, Z-dorm counselor, expressed dismay when he learned that Lackey (residents) was told of his return to the hall. Don firmly conveyed, "you should never tell these guys that you're takin' 'em to the hall!!!...Because they take other resident's belongings; you know it (belongings) just walks right out of here." Likewise, Shari opposes *telling residents* because of their likelihood to awol. She maintains, "I've seen too many residents awol when they found out they were going to the hall. If you really want them to go to the hall, you shouldn't tell them. But if you want them to awol, tell 'em." Instead, this group supports disguising their intent. A resident may be told that he is going on a "purchase order" (to buy clothing) or on a family conference, but residents are significantly surprised when they discover and/or end-up at Central Juvenile Hall. Don and Shari are speaking to the classic problem of managing residents (inmates generally) "between control structures" (Emerson,1969:211). Both Don and Shari prefer deception but disguising intent also serves to reduce anxiety and decrease resistance by residents. Those residents who are deceived by purchase order or family conference often put up less struggle or no struggle.

Those staff who support *telling residents* do so out of "fairness." Marcus (W-dorm social worker) believes that it is "only fair" to inform residents of their situation, giving them an opportunity to modify their behavior. Inga (intake worker/administrator) admits that her rationale behind *telling residents* is to identify a reaction to determine whether such a resident is suitable to return. Moreover, her reason for sending them to juvenile hall concerns the resident's need for "time-out," e.g., "they need time-out from placement. They need to see how easy they have it here." Kiman (male), night counselor, regards *telling residents* as a treatment issue; he maintains, "I wouldn't want to trick them because they don't learn anything from tricking them. And you know, they might become less trusting of you and the program." Finally, Marcus believes that "you should come straight out of the pump and tell the kid...You see, because these kids know the program, they know the boundaries, they know the rules, so why should I lie to them?"

While the above staff recognized that *telling residents* could cause fights between residents, resistance toward staff or resident awoling, their choice to tell residents reflects an honest frankness, and having authority to enforce their decision. It also suggest that they are willing to undergo any inconveniences (fights, staff disrespect) that results from telling residents. This type of staff is often concerned not only with the resident's well being but the entire dorm atmosphere. Lying to residents could in fact effect the trust level of residents towards staff and the overall credibility of the program.

Transporting Residents to Juvenile Hall: Between Control Structures

Staff who transport residents to juvenile hall are "between control structures" (Emerson, 1969:211). That is while taking a resident from OBH to JH any number of problems could occur. Frequently, staff are concerned with how to manage residents "between control structures". The transition appears difficult in that residents have been terminated to a lock down facility. If residents reject the "be good and return to OBH" proposition, then residents may reason that they have nothing to lose by awoling, jumping out of the van or taking out some long held frustrations on certain staff (by fighting, cursing or spitting on staff).

OBH has devised a strategy to ease staff fears and combat resident misbehavior during the transportation process. Technically then, no less than three staff are to accompany any one resident to juvenile hall. One staff drives while the resident is positioned two seats behind the driver on the door-less side of the van. One staff is positioned next to the resident and the final staff is positioned directly behind the driver (in front of the resident), facing the resident. The major function of the non-drivers are to ensure the safety of the resident and driver, e.g., restrain residents who attempt to attack the driver, harm themselves and/or exit the van when in motion.

Increasingly, this technical and structural policy only happens in ideal situations. Most times, there is a shortage of staff, causing staff to improvise their transporting scheme. My research uncovered a variety of ways in which residents were transported to juvenile hall. For example, OBH recruits and accepts residents from as far away as Alameda County, and when these residents are terminated, it is logistically difficult to transport them in the usual way. Consequently, OBH staff transports residents to Burbank airport, checks them in at the ticket counter, walks them to the departure area, sits with them until boarding time, watches them board and leaves after the plane has taken flight. The resident flies into Alameda County, meeting his probation officer at the airport. This probation officer then transports the resident to juvenile hall. Clearly, there are times when this arrangement has not worked smoothly, e.g., flight arrivals are mal-communicated and probation officers never arrives, causing residents to call parents for pick-up. Or, the resident simply awols. But in most cases, this plan works well therefore the practice remains.

There are several cases in which only two staff accompanied a resident to juvenile hall; and there are fewer cases when staff have had no other alternative except to use a poorly operating, compact size Datsun station wagon. One uses the Datsun when there is no other vehicle, preferably a van, available. Clearly this automobile is a "last resort" vehicle and its usage is an indication that social workers (and others) are anxious to relief themselves of their "problem child."

The danger of only two staff accompanying residents to juvenile hall is apparent when escapes occur. Seemingly, the resident likelihood of "acting-out" is greater and staff worry is increased. When Raymond and Ricardo transported Mata (resident) to juvenile hall, they were concerned about when and how Mata would make his great escape. Raymond reasoned that Mata would flee at a stoplight, but he did not. According to Raymond, "Mata waited until we drove up into the drive way of San Bernardino Juvenile Hall, then opened the van door and ran off." Clearly, *two staff accompaniment* is a very serious concern for staff and the reality of Mata awoling further heightens the risk and suspense of these situations. Certain staff, justifiably question the safety of this *two staff practice*. Practically though, staff who work in other dorms (not associated with "terminatee") and available staff are typically recruited, if needed, to assist in transporting residents.

Staff experiences while transporting residents to juvenile hall are varied. Staff may have smooth transitions from placement to juvenile hall, for clearly some residents chose "the hall" over awoling because of their opportunity to return. Thus their behavior, during the transportation process, is a major factor for reconsideration and re-admittance. But all trips to juvenile hall are not necessarily problem free. Garr (recreation staff) conveyed that he drove the van that transported McDowell (resident) to the hall. According to Garr, it took five Opportunity staff to restrain McDowell in the van; while traveling, McDowell was so aggressively angry that he spat on each staff member, receiving no retaliation. Garr then imagined himself as one of the staff who was spat upon, boasting, "If McDowell had of spit on me, I would have spit back or hit back."

Similarly, Kiman recalls that "we had to restrain Batiste (resident); it was a big scuffle. He was cursin' us and shit because he was mad that he was going to the hall." Kevin's juvenile hall experience was also physical. His sweater was torn in their (Kevin and Rone, staff) "tussle to get Woodson (resident) in the van." But once in the van Kevin relates how he performs his own control strategy:

"When I got in the van, I sat by the door. I always sit by the door. I strapped in Woodson's seat belt and locked the door. I never strap my seat beat because if I have to tussle with a kid, I don't want to be worried about unstrappin' a seat beat...Woodson was tellin' me, 'I don't know why I'm goin' to the hall? The staff's always fuckin' with me; Inga's always fuckin' with me!' I would talk to him and try to calm him down...I'd tell him if his behavior is good in the hall, then he would be back. I told him how he was messin' up and these people wouldn't send him to the hall if he wasn't. So then it would come to him that he'd been messin' up."

In contrast, Mark is not nearly as control conscious as Kevin. Mark more or less challenged Gomez (resident) by daring him to jump: "I'm goin' 60 to 60 mph; and I told him if he wanted to jump out of the van, go ahead and go!" At first glance, it may appear that Mark has little concern for control. But the dare to jump at such speed is one of the "mind games" (McDermott & King, 1988) played on residents by staff to in fact control a specific action, e.g., jumping out of the van. Very few persons, including residents, will jump from vans "goin' 60 to 80 mph."

Those residents who act out "between control structure" yet remain in the van, until it reaches juvenile hall, often change their demeanor and personality. Amusingly, Garr said, "as soon as we arrived inside the gates of juvenile hall, hall officials were signaled because we thought we might have a problem with McDowell." Three Central Juvenile Hall employees came to assist, but it turns out that they were not needed "because he (McDowell) straightened up and didn't cause any problems." Kiman (staff) was stunned at how "his (resident) attitude changed." Kiman speculated, "I think he knew the staff. Once we got to the hall, Batiste straightened up. He saw a staff that I think he knew and he started saying 'yes sir,' giving them all the respect. They didn't have near the scuffle we had." This changing of attitude and demeanor is also true for Taylor (resident) who claimed that he would put up a fight if staff took him to juvenile hall. Yet when arriving at juvenile hall Taylor was very cooperative. And Allen (staff) reports that when they arrived, Marlowe (resident) became very emotional, crying and begging Allen to reconsider. Finally, Mark revealed that "once we got to the hall, some of them were nervous; I could see it in their faces."

Arriving at juvenile hall, the transition is complete, ceasing interim control. Here, residents are departing a familiar set of staff and milieu, approaching a lock-down total institution in which most residents possess knowledge of how it operates. They recognize a clear difference between "the Hall" and "Opportunity", and this difference may account for abrupt behavior modifications. The rules of the game are different, and one does not want personal or technical fouls seconds into the game.

Returning from JH to OBH: Process and Staff Thoughts

Threatening to send residents back to juvenile hall is often a tactic used by staff to modified unacceptable residential behavior. When threats are used, staff seem more open to the resident's return (to OBH). In contrast, some staff become so frustrated with residents that they are beyond threats, wanting to get rid of the resident, period. In such cases, staff are less open for X-resident's return. Threats then suggest that there is room for improvement, whereby staff who have given up on certain residents are beyond threats, questioning the feasibility of their return.

The process of returning residents from juvenile hall to OBH is less stressful and more bureaucratic. Initially a bed-space must be available or becoming available soon. A resident might be scheduled to graduate on Friday and the returnee or new residents could be placed (at OBH) a day or two in advance. The probation officer of returnee is notified by OBH intake worker, of the Home's decision to return his client. In turn, the probation officer notifies the child's parents. Next, OBH staff typically drives to various hall location(s), obtaining the necessary paper work (resident's file and release documents) and interview returnees.[3] Interviews are often superficial in that they are part of the return process, staff are expected to return with X-resident and residents have been notified by probation officers of their placement and sometimes prepared as what to say during interviews. Mark (staff) explained, "when I interviewed John (returnee), he knew what to say. I went through the procedures 'cause they wanted to bring him back." Along with written documentation, Mark receives a verbal report from juvenile hall counselors responsible for returnees (John). And it is quite routine for OBH counselors to inquire about the returnee's behavior during juvenile hall detention.

Finally, the resident's release, the walk to the van and the trip to Opportunity. Here again, we are "between control structures" yet the concerns with control are less apparent given that one staff frequently returns residents. Residents are now behaviorally promoted, not demoted. Staff do not expect "tussles" or "scuffles", in fact, a different type of physical contact occurs, e.g., a handshake. According to Shari, many returnees were "relaxed" and not nervous: "Allot of those guys were inquisitive; they asked a ton of questions. Because once they get outside the gate [of JH], they seem more relaxed." Staff too are more relaxed in these situations, given their job is to take returnees Home. Given ones return, staff anticipates and depends on a certain level of self-control by residents. Staff control is also exhibited in his or her instructions given and followed by residents. For returnees, there is some familiarity with staff, residents, and place of destination; so conforming to role expectations not only eases the control process, but begins a new residential program for returnees.

"Between control structures," staff respond to questions by returnees about old acquaintances and new situations. Control was also made simpler by resident enthusiasm about leaving juvenile hall. Kevin (counselor) viewed them as "excited because they had been locked up for four or five months; they were glad to get out." Likewise, Mike (counselor) expressed that "some of them would say, 'I'm glad I'm getting' out of here (JH), so I can get my program together and go home." These comments suggest a certain excitement by residents who are returning. At this point, residents seem less interested in risking promotion, and more interested in discovering and participating in their new environment. An unspecified norm of control by residents and staff seems at work. Again, it is a self-control that longs for the opportunity to experience "freedom" and exercise more choices.

Residents who return from juvenile hall (to OBH) receive mixed reviews by staff. By in large, social workers and administrators favor resident returns, arguing that the juvenile hall experience changes their behavior. Conversely, line staff (counselors, case aides, dorm-coordinators) largely object to resident returns, maintaining that the return process is ambiguous, and returns are "counter productive." Line staff clearly have more social contact with residents than social workers and administrators. Administrative evaluations are based on periodic contact[4], verbal and written information from line staff. Line staff opinions stem directly from continuous, everyday interaction.

If, for example, we accept the contention by line staff that juvenile hall "returnees" are "counter productive" and less likely to succeed, how might this be explained? Upon return, the relationships among returnees and their friends has not changed; peers and friends often expect returnees to resume their "old self." Yet, staff monitors and expects behavioral changes. Having established a certain role and self identity, returnees usually fall into similar relationships with peers, permitting their past delinquent behavior to re-surface. Socially, the difficulty of producing a better "program" becomes a significant challenge. Consider, for instance, the following observation:

> Recently, Sonny and Mitch (both X-dorm residents) returned from juvenile hall. Their behavior however has steadily declined. It is as if they never absorbed the juvenile hall experience, and present little concern for returning to juvenile hall. Their effect on residents also seems negative. Thus, it might be logical (and produce better results) to place "returnees" in other dorms, instead of their dorm of origin.

The above observation questions the resident return process along with returning residents to their original dorm. Many staff have raised similar inquiries and pondered the ambiguous return process. That is, given clinical concerns of the entire Home, what constitutes solid grounds for allowing a resident to return? Peacefully returning to juvenile hall? An available dorm opening? Probation officers pleading for their clients? Chronologically, residents who go to juvenile hall without physically resisting or awoling often have a better chance of returning than otherwise. Next, an available bed space is a necessary condition before one can return. Here, when residential population is low, OBH is not as clinically selective. Administrators seek to maintain their population cap; low population reduces OBH's overall capital intake. Lastly, probation officers have made "last chance" pleads for their clients whose behavior was so poor that no other placement would accept them. Are these grounds on which OBH accepts and admits returnees? Or, as many staff insinuate, OBH is a business, they are more concerned about "filling bed spaces and maintaining pop" than treatment. In short, the return policy is unclear and has never been explicitly spelled out; the arbitrary nature of the return process has nevertheless caused many staff to reject it altogether.

Mara, for instance, concludes that returning residents from juvenile hall is detrimental to other residents, sending a "double message" to all residents. Residents would take the program more seriously if terminated inmates were not allowed to return. Additionally, residents receive a message that its O.K. to "mess up" for they are conscious of their most severe penalty (juvenile hall), "but if they play the system right, there is a good chance of their return." Consequently, Mara believes that returning terminated residents is "counter productive," suspecting that treatment is not the central concern for administrators. Instead, the economics of servicing a complete residential population and the politics of probation officer relationships appears most significant.[5]

Mara's sentiments result from the vague return policy as well as residents who return, becoming more burdensome and problematic. For example, Boyles returned from juvenile hall, was placed in a new dorm, but eventually fought with staff. Pires returned, and was alleged to have a "female minor in dorm (room)," leading him to awol for fear of returning to the hall; Taylor, has gone and returned from juvenile hall several times. Many staff then, disagree with resident returns while others are more objective, believing that returnees are situational. That is, under what conditions was X-resident terminated? And is OBH capable of treating X-resident's social problems? Whatever the reason, returnees tend to do worst than others, while the lack of an explicit policy further confuses residents and staff, which seemingly undermines the whole premise of treatment at OBH.

There are however several successful juvenile hall returns, but the problematic returns seem to overshadow those who return problem free. Administrator Inga conveys, "while they're there (in the Hall), they see the judge, and he reads them the riot act before the kid gets back....If a kid has judge Horn (Horn has a reputation for being heavy-handed), he has to face him in the hall, before he gets back to placement." This remark then assumes that changing one's environment elicits behavioral changes (when returned to placement). Maldonado, for example, is a resident that turned his program around, almost immediately, upon his juvenile hall return. Maldonado's case is atypical because other residents who have returned and eventually display progress, have not changed at such a rapid pace. Consider this observation:

> Maldonado is doing very well; that is, he appears to have a respectful attitude towards staff, he rarely horseplays, and now, Maldonado is working in the kitchen. Clearly, he has turned his program around.

Maldonado then is a case in point for administrators and social workers who argue that the hall experience changes their behavior. The behavioral changes of "the Maldonados" functions, in part, to justify the return process and still ulterior motives by administration are usually suspected by subordinate staff.

Finally, there are practical and clinical reasons for returning residents from juvenile hall to OBH. One practical matter is whether a dorm opening exists. According to Maggie, one major reason for McVay's (resident) return to V-dorm centered around the availability of space. Clinically though, Maggie maintained that V-dorm staff would not accept a resident in which they could not meet his needs. For instance, "a strong Black resident that needed a strong Black male figure would not be suitable to return to V-dorm," given V-dorm staff had no African American male. Unfortunately, clinical practices are typically inconsistent; and though Maggie prefers to work with "suitable" residents, there are varying circumstances when residential dorm assignments are involuntary. Space availability, on the other hand, is a very real consideration, particularly when dorms are under-populated.

Though juvenile hall, in part, functions as a control mechanism, the extent to which it impacts residents is debatable. The inconsistent usage of juvenile hall has led staff to question whether it is really a behavioral deterrent. Counselors, social workers and administrators clearly possess varying views; but it is administrators and social workers who wield the most power. Many line staff resent returning residents, and often, lack inclusion regarding return decisions. For better or worst, most return decisions are made by administrators and social workers, while line staff are charged with counseling, monitoring and maintaining control of residents.

Summary

Awols and terminations focus on leaving the facility, either voluntarily or involuntarily. Awols indicate that residents leave without permission, while residents who are terminated are forced to leave. Most awolees return, giving staff more leverage over the resident's behavior and future at OBH. Returning awolees who fail or refuse to adhere to program standards are ultimately terminated. Termination, or sending residents to juvenile hall is the harshest and final instance of control available to staff. In short, termination is a last resort option.

The open, community-based nature of OBH is often tempting to residents who contemplate awoling. Those who ponder awoling usually fall into five general categories, e.g., injustice, terminal, avoidance, lonesome, and sneaky thrill awols. These awol categories or awol types are developed from accounts and excuses given by residents to staff. Staff then receives awol accounts, constructing their version of residential awols.

The awol process guides us through various steps of an awol as viewed by staff. Our examination of the Duran, Mata and Brown cases reveal that each awol has a life of its own. And while Duran eventually decided against awoling, the Mata and Brown awols reflect terminal type awols. The "return process" has a tendency to humble residents in that returnees are willing to confess their mistakes and rightfully accept punishment. The return process involves five stages, e.g., **searching, questioning, instruction, counseling** and **sanctioning**.

Juvenile hall is considered the worst and most severe sanction applied to residents. It is in fact a last resort response to maintaining control and restoring order. "The hall" signifies placement failure; it is a type of downward mobility that transfers one from an open facility to a lock-down total institution. In keeping with treatment philosophies, residents who remain in placement and placement staff do not attach negative labels to residents who fail placement. Sometimes, residents are unable to adjust to OBH, other times, residents are said to need "time out" from placement.

Residents who cannot adjust to OBH are not likely to return; yet residents who require "time out" may in fact return. The fact that returning is an option for terminated residents—does not sit well with some staff. On the one hand, opponents to *juvenile hall returns* maintain that it is counter-productive in that it sends "double messages" to all residents. Conversely, supporters of *juvenile hall returns* contend that the juvenile hall experience changes their behavior, giving them more appreciation for placement. Whatever the case, whether one leaves by awol or termination, community-based treatment programs frequently provide second chances .

Notes

1.   Review the Brown and Mata cases, previous chapter.

2.   Again, review the Brown case, previous chapter.

3.   All returnees are not interviewed. The intake worker, Inga, may instruct staff not to interview due to her familiarity with returnees.

4.   When administrators have residential contact, it is usually positive; residents typically present their "good side," their best self.

5.   When residential capacity is full, OBH is paid maximally. Also, good P.O. relations could result in the admittance of a higher quality, better behaved resident, making staff and administrative work easier.

Chapter 8

Afterthoughts

In the final analysis, using a social control framework illuminates the nature of staff work at OBH. Staff work involves varying types of human encounters with juvenile residents. These encounters define the structure of resident/staff interactions. Staff, of course, have institutional authority, and can rely on punishment and rules to guide residents' behavior. But even this institutional power alone cannot ensure conformity. Staff thus must actively engage in control-work, i.e., deciding when and where to enforce institutional rules, when to accomplish conformity by some other means, and when to look the other way.

This study has shown how staff implement social control in varying styles. *Control variance* among staff is due to the inevitable use of discretion in people work. It is difficult to practice **judicial objectivity** (giving everyone the same punishments for similar infractions) when applying sanctions to residents. Rather control-work must be flexible to match the unpredictable and situational nature of residential violations.

My analysis of social control examined variations in staff members' judgments when defining deviant behavior. Social control requires two key stages, definition and response. These stages rely on staff/resident encounters, often producing reactive responses by staff. Gibbs reminds us that "a particular act is deviant, if and only if, it is reacted to distinctively ... by at least one member of the social unit in question" (1981:25).

The objective of **learning control** was to examine how staff learned, interpreted and understood their work. We discovered how staff learn by formal training, watching, doing, making mistakes, receiving instruction from experienced staff, and receiving instruction from residents. Interestingly, as new staff begin, they learn that their work primarily involves control, e.g., establishing and maintaining order. Those who acquire good control skills are perceived as "strong staff," receiving more dorm responsibility and respect from residents and staff. Staff having difficulty with control are viewed as "weak," receiving less control responsibility and less respect from residents and staff.

Staff definitions and reactions to deviant behavior were clearly evident in **everyday control**. Staff are responsible for defining and responding to their perceptions of deviance. As in **everyday control**, the purpose of *situational remedies* is to correct minor wrongdoings immediately, without punishment. Conversely, *institutional remedies* were linked to more serious rule violations, which were handled through formal institutional procedures, and agents outside the situation.

Invoking situational remedies is a key process for staff, in that they define situations, determine wrongdoing and correct violations. Staff situational responses to troubles are often spontaneous, and in some cases reactive. For example, when Misty (staff) witnessed a "milk infraction," she immediately ordered Wynn (resident) to "put it back!!" It was a minor violation, with a quick encounter, and a rapid resolution.

Alternatively, institutional remedies are more complex and have longer-term, broader implications. The key distinctions between situational remedies and institutional remedies concern types of infractions, formal punishment, written documentation and a likelihood of external staff involvement. A fight among residents is likely to produce an institutional response. This incident requires possible assistance from other staff, documentation and formal punishment.

It is clear that *situational remedies* and *institutional remedies* occur outside corrections. For instance, in the case of *situational remedies*, young teenagers caught sneaking into movie theatres are ordered by managers to leave or pay. School teachers experience *institutional remedies* when student violations are referred to the principle's office. Authority figures, regardless of social setting, react to certain rule violations. Their reaction verifies the existence and reality of certain social structures.

The **panic button** examined how staff actually responded to institutional emergencies. It critically analyzed how staff restored order in crisis situations. Crisis situations suggest that severe troubles exist and that assistance is needed. No matter the crisis, controlling problems are central, returning OBH to some sense of normality.

In part then, I focused on formal control strategies to restore order during emergencies. Developing and maintaining formal control strategies, in response to emergencies, is significant, for it gives staff a "blueprint" on how to respond. Blueprints however are frequently altered, as are formal control strategies to restore order during emergencies. People work implies a type of situational modification; and outcomes frequently create informal control techniques in managing emergencies. In the absence of OBH officials and certain staff, informal techniques clearly emerge, primarily because various formal techniques may not work.

Sociologically, correctional institutions are little different from other institutions regarding emergencies. That is, families, churches, summer camps, schools, businesses and transportation agencies all exhibit formal and inform strategies of handling crises. Crises are indeed social facts that are usually unpredictable, but no less require attention. The type of attention heightens our consciousness of what is occurring. OBH is one of many institutions that responds to emergencies, e.g., crises that are specific to community-base group homes.

Finally, **leaving** gets at awoling, which is voluntary, and termination, which is involuntary. Leaving is directly or indirectly tied to processes of control. For instance, when awolees return, they have little room for negotiation; thus awolees are more receptive to instruction and control. Alternatively, residents who are given every opportunity to conform but refuse are controlled by termination. Such **leavings** (awol and termination) are specific to Opportunity Boys' Home, but one could locate certain qualities of correctional leaving in other institutions, e.g., school, work and the sport industry.

Again, **leaving** is a most interesting control mechanism. That is, if the "problem" leaves (e.g., leaves a boys' home, a school, an occupation, an athletic team, etc), there is little need to control that individual; his departure has, in part, solved one's immediate control dilemma. To a certain extent, the individual's lack of conformity no longer effects others, making dorm or work conditions more manageable for authorities. Here, **leaving** is examined in reference to Opportunity Boys' Home, e.g., corrections. However, the idea of leaving is further relevant to students leaving classrooms (or schools), workers leaving jobs, players leaving athletic teams, teenagers leaving homes, wives leaving husbands and slaves leaving plantations. The primary difference between OBH residents and others is that the latter are not bound by court orders, but by different types of constraints. The real issue is control; when one is unhappy with his social circumstance, the choice to leave is real, and many take this option. In part, leaving suggest that subordinates no longer honor control by their situational superiors; subordinates wish to take their lives into their own hands, e.g., a type of individual autonomy. While leaving a job, a classroom, a plantation or home is not awoling, workers, students, teenagers and slaves leave on their own accord, without permission. When and if workers, students, teenagers and slaves return, there are usually "consequences" (punishments).

Additionally, problem residents who resist conformity or OBH contracts are forced to leave, sent away against their will. The consequences of termination, return to juvenile hall, has ways of producing desired results, e.g., conformity. Few residents seek deprivation of Home privileges and amenities. In similar ways, workers, students and slaves who are control problems and fail to conform are typically forced to leave. Unruly workers are fired, cheating students are dismissed and revolutionary slaves are traded, sold or killed. Exhausting all control remedies, authority figures seek to maintain control by using "final straw" measures.

The final twist to the *leaving metaphor* is one's ability to actually leave. Goffman's (1961) analysis of total institutions suggests that one cannot leave (mental institutions or prisons), but work and living occur in an isolated area. Here, authorities place restrictions on leaving and actively prevent escapes. Conversely, as an institutional form, the group home is "quasi-total." The "quasi" quality evolves from its openness, and in this environment, staff are not required to prevent "leavings."

It follows that community-based institutions have integrated corrections with communities. They are no longer isolated, nor perceived as "junior jails." Communities that include group homes may break stereotypic assumptions about corrections and their clients. For example, when group homes are established in communities, it is very likely that certain group home residents will attend similar public schools as resident youth of that community. And by being in communities (neighborhoods, school, church), observations and interactions occur that could lead to friendships and better understanding of group home systems.

Still, the corrections community knows little about community-based institutions like Opportunity Boys' Home. More research, using ethnographies, surveys, and experiments, is needed. Current research (Kobrin & Klein, 1983) on community-based institutions seem primarily interested in recidivism, asking whether community based institutions are more successful than state run institutions. I contend that success rates are not the only issue. We must know how community-based institutions *really* work. Exactly, what are their limitations? And how can communities become more informed and involved in community based institutions?

Finally, services delivered by community-based institutions are improved as we acquire more knowledge about these facilities. Such information helps judges in their referral of juveniles, and legislators in their writing and enactment of juvenile legislation. More than that, judges, legislators, parents, probation officers and social workers desire alternatives to state run institutions. Generally, community-based institutions provide additional choices. Options may further have treatment implications for residents; that is, residents in state-run institutions may desire similar autonomy and amenities accorded community-based residents. They may feel a sense of "autonomy-amenity deprivation." If so, the behavior of juveniles in state-run institutions may change, making them eligible for community-based opportunities, e.g., placement in community-based group homes.

Appendix

Research Methods and Charts

Role of Researcher

During any participant observation study, information received from informants largely depends on the perception of one's status, and the intentions of the researcher. Gathering significant data, developing trust, comfort and cooperation among subjects takes time (Jorgensen, 1989; Johnson, 1975). Unlike Horowitz (1989), my research role did not develop with the usual "break the ice, get-to-know-you" routine. I was *native*, e.g., I was employed, initially as a recreation assistant, then a dorm counselor, then night counselor and finally an O.D. I was an "insider" (Jorgensen, 1989:60); I knew people, the OBH system and varying situations before formally engaging in research.[1] Thus, after taking a graduate course in ethnography and needing fresh data for a dissertation, I decided to continue my fieldwork.

My research role is best described as "participant-as-observer." Here, "the field worker's observer activities are not wholly concealed, but are 'kept under wraps'"(Junker, 1960:36). Essentially, some knew of my research and others did not. Specific others who knew, did not share this knowledge. My research role was very similar to Brenda Mann's, of *The Cocktail Waitress* (1975), who was employed by her research site (as was I); and while some knew she was conducting research, many did not.

Hence, employment at the research site makes one more of an insider, but it does not make you native. One could become native, but this too is a process. Mann (1975) was an insider and "pressured to go native" but refused. My OBH employment career and involvement positioned me as native and an insider; so when I decided to do research few knew my new role. In fact, those who knew frequently assisted in obtaining documents and concealing my status.

Having a 3.5 years stock of knowledge before formally engaging in fieldwork posed possible "recognition" and "insensitivity" problems (for myself).[2] That is, I was aware and concerned about overlooking incidents, taking others for granted and becoming insensitive to the setting. Apparently, being cognizant of my knowledge stock had the opposite affect. That is, I became very sensitive and focused on familiar problems, examining everyday occurrences in ways that broaden my analysis.

My role and status as O.D. permitted me to investigate various situations thoroughly. For example, I extensively observed and examined social interaction among line staff (dorm coordinators, case aides & dorm counselors), social workers, residents, and administrators in varying places and situations, e.g., dorms, O.D. office, gym, kitchen, group sessions, crisis situations, playing fields, field trips, staff meetings, nurse's office, OBH chapel, OBH school, OBH dances and transporting residents to juvenile hall.

For nearly three years, I recorded extensive field notes, permitting certain issues to develop, and comparing instances one to another. Being a "participant-as-observer" allowed me to participate, observe unsuspect-ingly, conduct unstructured interviews,[3] converse with most staff, and examine official documents (incident reports, awol reports and OBH main log & dorm logs) written by staff.[4] Given my O.D. status, my role was "provided by the setting," e.g., "insider roles are provided by the setting" (Jorgenson, 1989:60). And during my encounters, the extent to which I was perceived as O.D. was largely situational. For instance, when residents returned from awol or providing formal information to new staff, I was clearly viewed as O.D. Conversely, as I engaged in casual talk with other staff about insensitive administrators, poor pay and clocking-out others, I was viewed as "just another staff" or a friend. Needless to say, in both situations, I used my status to obtain information.

In his book, *Doing Field Research*, Johnson (1975) discusses "the increasing importance of official records." Johnson argues that one significant result of official records was the "development of a close association between the daily work of social workers and the perceived necessity for documenting this work" (1975:44). In my case, official documents (incident reports, awol reports, OBH main log and dorm logs) proved extremely useful in determining certain inconsistencies among staff written reports and actual behavior. It was also interesting to note how some incident reports were over-reported and others, under-reported.[5] Moreover, awol reports provided official reasons for resident awols. Thus, awol reports combined with self-reports (from residents), resulted in a "typology of awols" (see chapter on "Resident Leaving: Awoling").

I gathered data on issues related to learning control, everyday control, panic button (or Home emergencies), and leaving (awol or termination) the institution. Regarding learning control, I frequently attended in-service training sessions for new staff. Here, I observed partial and entire training sessions. At times, I reflected on my own in-service training as a new staff, wondering whether formal research (surveys or ethnographies) had ever been conducted. In other situations, I observed new staff in action, e.g., line-ups, emergencies, staff confrontations with residents, group sessions. I participated in some of these activities and later (sometimes spontaneously) talked with new staff about their experiences.

Compiling information on everyday control was most interesting, for here is a chapter that examines how staff do control daily. Everyday control examines the daily routines of staff and how they respond to minor and serious infractions. Few staff responded to violations in similar ways, but responses often reflect the incident and the situation.

Collecting data on the panic button (emergencies) was usually quite fruitful. When emergency buttons or panic buttons sounded, I ran to the emergency scene, as did other staff. The act of being there and participating makes for lots of interesting and emerging information. The idea is to control the crisis. Responding to emergencies frequently means breaking up fights and settling dorms. As researcher, I appreciated how information naturally emerged through talk, watching others, listening to others (counselors, social workers, residents), asking questions during and after emergencies and reading official reports and log entries on emergencies.

Collecting data on leaving examined two types of departures, e.g., awoling and terminations to juvenile hall. In both instances, one gains extreme insight by participating in the leaving experience of residents. That is, by watching and questioning residents as they pack, then awol, or driving a resident to juvenile hall and being present when residents are formally told of their termination. Participant-as-observer allowed me to participate by being on the scene, thus questioning and discussing with residents their awol and juvenile hall experiences. I informally interviewed staff about their thoughts on residents who awol; other times, staff blurted out their angry or joyous thoughts upon learning of a resident's awol and termination.

As O.D., I would characterize myself as "the peoples' O.D." Most subjects (social workers, counselors, residents) appeared at ease when sharing information. Sometimes, staff desired relief from stressful dorms, thus came to the O.D. office for relaxing conversations. Here, according to Jorgensen (1989), I was in a natural position to obtain information and raise unsuspecting questions. The few who were apprehensive often prefaced their response with: "keep this to yourself" or "you didn't hear it from me, but..."

Additionally, subjects felt comfortable because not only was I easy to talk with, but I played the appropriate role at the proper time. When Lawney Shawn (kitchen staff) stole food, I did not inform administrators because we had formed a good friendship and it was simple to cover up. When staff clocked out early and for others, I turned the other way, informing no one, for it had little effect on others. In short, then, I became (or was) one of "them," as oppose the morning O.D., who was not one of "them." She was perceived as rigid and anxious, consequently, many staff used careful language when conversing in her presence. She appeared too loyal to administrators, e.g., frequently in their offices, giving detailed verbal reports, snitching on employees who were late and sometimes scolding fellow staff.

Administrators then, believed that I could manage and control the Home. I knew what to do, I knew how to handle crises, when to be calm and when to be forceful. I knew what to write, what to omit and what to tell administrators. I handled their requests and demands. As much as one could be trusted, I was trusted, initially. This position requires a certain confidence that one can get the job done, and perceived loyalty to administration. Initially, much information about staff, residents, etc. was reported to meet their (administration's) expectations. I made certain recommendations (e.g., getting rid of on-site security guards and having night staff be more security conscious; also recommending that certain staff live in on campus apartments) that were endorsed and implemented.

As with most social encounters, one's relationship with others changes through time, conditions and circumstances (Johnson, 1975). For example, when licensing conducted two surprise inspections within six months, it was rumored (through Janette's secretary) that some "disgruntled staff must have called licensing because they knew to go straight to the nurse's office."[6] When dents were discovered on Home vehicles but not formally reported, the Executive Director's suspicion of all staff involved was heightened. These situations strained Henry (Executive Director) from telling me of certain staff he suspected or the intimate details of licensing citations, e.g., the magnitude and quantity of citations, which he freely revealed before. Henry believed that I should have known and reported these instances to him.

These were some of the major drawbacks of being an O.D., e.g., rumors hurled in your direction and Henry's suspicion and sometimes unrealistic expectations of O.D.s, e.g., that they should know *everything!* This eased the flow of confidential information that normally sprung from Henry, but it did not distract from gathering data from other staff on learning control, emergencies, awoling and terminations. We (line staff) participated in most of these instances together. Admittedly though, residents were sometimes reluctant and vague in explaining why they awoled and their reasons for return. Such residents perceived me as an authority figure who might participate-in and influence their punishment.

By working at OBH, as O.D., I was in an advantageous position to obtain information. Entering the parking lot, and searching for a parking space, essentially began my research day. Whatever I saw or heard could be recorded. Casual conversations with any member of the OBH community could prove useful. So information flowed and was gathered in various ways. For example, sometimes I performed strictly as O.D. and noted what occurred after my shift, or when I had a private moment during my shift. Other times, I performed strictly as O.D., but asked research questions after an incident. Such questions were unsuspecting in that subjects (respondents) could not distinguish between "research questions" and "O.D. questions." Information from "O.D. questions" was documented in the main log, dorm log or documented on official forms, e.g., incident report or awol report. But information received from "research questions" may have been documented in both my field notes and OBH official records. And there were many times when information from "research questions" was only placed in field notes.

There were even times when I asked "pure" research questions, e.g., questions I would not have asked had I simply been the O.D. Likewise, I observed situations (staff learning, resident/staff encounters, the panic button process, etc) more keenly and critically as researcher, not as O.D.

Again, this gets at the advantages of "insiders" and points to the availability of immense data in environments where researchers are employed. I systematically collected incident reports, awol reports, and noted relevant issues from logs. This, I would have never done had it not been for my research objective. And my position allowed access to all such documentation. I did not have to ask to see or read incident/awol reports; they were at my disposal, e.g., all incident and awol reports are submitted to the O.D. office, first. Then, they are distributed to administrators.

Seemingly, it would be more difficult, but not impossible, for outsiders (county licensing inspectors, politicians, probations officers) to learn about the rare instances of unreported child abuse, the details of false alarms, staff clocking out for one another, staff mistakes, staff learning styles, staff theft and incident report writing, e.g., information included and excluded. Conversely, administrators, social workers, dorm counselors and residents could learn about most of the aforementioned issues because they have access to a similar information flow, e.g., incident reports, awol reports, dorm logs, main log, groups sessions, staff and resident encounters. An administrator may not witness child abuse personally, but he or she might obtain information from secondary sources, or even a primary source, e.g., the resident, himself. Their interpretation is conceivably altered and then it becomes an issue of "his word against mine." Still administrators, counselors, and social workers have the ability to learn what I discovered because we share the same workspace; yet our research angles would diverge (Hammersley & Atkinson, 1983).

The diversity in my role responsibilities and methodologies allowed unsuspecting access to fruitful and rich data.[7] The issues that naturally emerged contain several instances for comparison and analysis. My methods are not new but the way I "fell" into this study gave me an edge on obtaining data, analyzing data and *really* feeling what other staff felt, e.g., I was truly one of *them*.

FRONTLINE-STAFF/RESIDENT POPULATION CHART

Dorm	Resident Census Per Dorm	Average Staff	Required Staff	
Dorm V	16	5	6	
Dorm W	12	4	5	
Dorm X	20	6	7	
Dorm Y	16	5	6	
Dorm Z	20	6	7	
5 Dorms	84	26	31	Totals

This chart does not include social workers or administrators. The chart identifies front-line staff (counselors, case aides, and dorm coordinators). Staffing may vary based on turnover rates; it is not unusual for Opportunity Boys' Home to be under-staffed.

Resident population also varies by awols, graduations and terminations. Licensing allows OBH to hold 84 residents. Resident allotments are determined by bed space.

Resident census per dorm and average staff numbers reflect OBH population as of January, 1990.

Required staff indicates that Licensing requires OBH to have 6 staff for a dorm (V) population of 16; and 5 staff for a dorm (W) population of 12, etc.

OPPORTUNITY BOYS'S HOME   AWOL REPORT

To: _____

Name of Resident: _____ AKA: _____

Staff Reporting Disappearance: _____

Location Last Seen: _____ Possible Destination: _____

Date of Disappearance: _____ Time: _____

Clothing Worn: _____ Medical Condition: _____

Substance Abuse: _____

L.A.P.D. Missing Juveniles Informed (485-2563) Date: ___ Time: _____

Parents Notified: Date _____ Time _____ By Whom _____

How? _____

Placement Officer Notified: Date ____ Time _____ By Whom _____

Circumstances Surrounding Disappearance: _____

_____

_____

Formal Report filed with LAPD.: Date __ Time __ Delivered By _____

IF RESIDENT IS LOCATED:

Where? _____ When? _____ By Whom? _____

If Detained: Where? _____ Date _____ Time _____ By Whom _____

IF RETURNED TO OPPORTUNITY HOME:

Date: _____ Time: _____ By Whom? _____

Placement Officer Notified: Date ___ Time __ By Whom _____

Parents Notified: Date _____ Time _____ By Whom? _____

Report cancelled (telephonic - formal) Date __ Time __ By Whom _____
                         (circle)

TERMINATION DATE _____

Drug-Abuse   Damage   Physical   Suicide   Medical   Other

Opportunity Boys' Home

Incident Report

Date of Incident _____

To: _____ From: _____ Report Date: _____

Incident Involved:_____

Observed By: Staff_____

Residents _____

Brief Description of Incident: _____

_____

_____

_____

_____

_____

OBH First Aid Required: _____ Describe: _____

Medical Attention: _____ Doctor/Hospital: _____

If off-grounds people involved, who, how, where? _____

_____

Immediate Action Taken: _____

_____

By Staff: _____

Resident's Statement: _____

Police Notified? _____ Parent Notified? _____ P.O. Notified? _____

_____

Signature

Notes

1.   I began collecting field notes in January 1987. In order to protect privacy of staff and residents, **all names are fictitious, as well as the facility (OBH).**

2.   See Jorgenson (1989) *Participant Observation;* he discusses how the researcher's "personal experience" in settings and situations are subject to even more critical examination than the other experiences of other members.

3.   I did not ask interviewees the same set of questions; but after an awol, for example, I would ask staff involved how they felt about awols in general and specific cases. I asked whether staff work was more manageable due to certain awolees. Then, I would probe given my responses. I conducted over thirty interviews though some staff were interviewed more than once. The purpose of the interview was to get at the incident at hand, e.g., reactions to awols, reactions to certain staff decision, reactions to panic button, etc.

4.   I read and reviewed nearly ninety incident reports per month, for twelve months. I examined and noted most of the incident reports that came through the O.D. office. I reviewed and noted nearly all the awol reports that I personally witnessed. Here, I was interested in comparing that which was written by staff, and what was said or not said by residents.

5.   See chapter on **Everyday Control** for complete analysis of incident reports.

6   There were many violations concerning medication distribution and medication documentation. O.D.s, nurses, and a few line staff (Mary-Ann [fill-in nurse] and others) are involved in distributing and logging resident medications.

7   See Patricia Adler et al (1986), "The Politics of Participation in Field Research," for an analysis of fieldworkers who are co-present and/or actively participate with members of settings they study.

Bibliography

Adler, Patricia, Peter Adler & E. Burke Rochford (1986). "The Politics of Participation in Field Research." *Urban Life* 14:363-376.

Ahern, James (1972). *Police in Trouble: Our Frightening Crisis in Law Enforcement*. New York: Hawthorn Books.

Asincof, Eliot, Warren Hinckle & William Turner (1973). *The 10-Second Jailbreak: The Helicopter Escape of Joel David Kaplan*. New York: Holt, Rinehart & Winston.

Ball, Richard, C. Ronald Huff & J. Robert Lilly (1988). *House Arrest & Correctional Policy: Doing Time at Home*. Beverly Hills: Sage Publication.

Bandura, Albert (1977). *Social Learning Theory*. Englewood Cliffs, New Jersey: Prentice-Hall.

Bartos, Otomar (1974). *Process and Outcome of Negotiations*. New York: Columbia University Press.

Bazer, Max and Margaret Neale (1992). *Negotiating Rationally*. New York: The Free Press.

Becker, Howard, Blanche Geer, Everett Hughes and Anselm Strauss (1961). *Boys in White: Student Culture in Medical School*. Chicago: University of Chicago Press.

Bennett, Lerone Jr. (1988). *Before the Mayflower: A History of Black America*, 6th. ed. New York: Penguin Books.

Birenbaum, Arnold, Samuel Seiffer (1976). *Resettling Retarded Adults in a Managed Community*. New York: Praeger Publishers.

Bittner, Egon (1974). "Esprit De Corps and the Code of Secrecy." J. Goldsmith and S. Goldsmith (eds.) in *The Police Community*. California: Palisades Publishers.

Black, Donald (1984). "Social Control as a Dependent Variable." In
      Towards a General Theory of Social Control, Volume 1:
      Fundamentals; New York: Academic Press.
Booth, Tim, Ken Simons and Wendy Booth (1990). *Outward Bound:*
      Relocation and Community Care for People with Learning
      Disabilities. Philadelphia: Open University Press.
Buckholdt, David and Jaber Gubrium (1979). *Caretakers: Treating*
      Emotionally Disturbed Children. Beverly Hills: Sage Publications.
Brown, Bert (1977). "Face-Saving and Face-Restoration in Negotiation."
      In D. Druckman (ed.) *Negotiations: Social-Psychological*
      Perspectives. Beverly Hills: Sage Publications.
Cicourel, Aaron (1974). *Cognitive Sociology: Language and Meaning in*
      Social Interaction. New York: Free Press.
Cohen, S. (1985). *Visions of Social Control.* MA: Polity Press.
Conklin, John (1972). *Robbery and the Criminal Justice System.*
      Philadelphia: Lippincott.
Coser, Lewis A. (1990). "Forced Labor in Concentrations Camps." In *The*
      Nature of Work: Sociological Perspectives. K. Erikson and S.P.
      Vallas, (eds.) New Haven: Yale Press.
Dance, Daryl C. (1978). *Long Gone: The Meckenburg Six of the Theme of*
      Escape in Black Folklore. Knoxville: University of Tennessee Press.
Denscombe, Martin (1985). *Classroom Control: A Sociological*
      Perspective. London: George Allen & Unwin.
de Kock, U, Felce, D., Saxby, H. & Thomas, M. (1987). "Staff Turnover in
      a Small Home Service: A Study of Facilities for Adults with severe and
      Profound Mental Handicaps." *Mental Handicap,* 15, pp. 97-101.
Emerson, Robert M. (1981). "On Last Resorts." *American Journal of*
      Sociology, 87:1-22.
_____. (1974). "Role Determinants in Juvenile Court," Daniel Glaser
      (ed.) In *Handbook of Criminology.* New York: Rand McNally College
      Publishing Company.
Empey, LaMar T. and Mark C Stafford (1991). *American Delinquency: Its*
      Meaning and Construction (3rd ed). Belmont: Wadsworth Publishing
      Company.
Frohboese, R. and B Sales (1980). "Parental Opposition to
      Deinstitutionalization." *Law and Human Behavior,* 4, 1/2, pp. 1-87.
Feld, Barry (1977). *Neutralizing Inmate Violence: Juvenile Offenders*
      in Institutions. Cambridge: Ballinger Publishing Company.

Gecas, Viktor (1981). "Contexts of Socialization." M. Rosenberg and R. Turner (eds.). In *Social Psychology: Sociological Perspectives*, New York: Basic Books.

Geertz, Clifford (1973). *The Interpretation of Cultures*. New York: Basic Books.

George, Linda L. (1983). "Nursing Turnover in Long-Term Care Institutions." Ida Simpson and Richard Simpson (eds.). In *Research in the Sociology of Work* Vol.2; Greenwich: JAI Press.

Gibbons, Don C. (1994). *Talking About Crime and Criminals*. New Jersey: Prentice-Hall.

Glaser, Daniel (1972). *Crime and Social Policy*. New Jersey: Prentice-Hall.

Goffman, Erving (1955). "On Face Work," *Psychiatry*, 18: 213-231.

_____. (1961). *Asylums: Essays on the Social Situation of Mental Patients and Other Inmates*. New York: Doubleday.

_____. (1974). *Frame Analysis*. New York: Harper & Row.

Gollay, Freedman, R. Wyngaarden, and Kurtz, N. (1978). *Coming Back: The Community Experiences of Deinstitutionalized Mentally Retarded People*. Cambridge, MA: Abt Books.

Halpern, J., Binner, P. Mohr, C., and Sackett, K. (1978). *The Illusion of Deinstitutionalization*. Denver Research Institute, Social Systems Research and Evaluation Division, University of Denver.

Hammersley, Martyn and Paul Atkinson (1983). *Ethnography: Principles in Practice*. London: Tavistock Publications.

Hasenfeld, Yeheskel (1983). *Human Service Organizations*. New Jersey: Prentice-Hall.

Heiss, Jerold (1981). "Social Roles." M. Rosenberg and R. Turner (eds.). In *Social Psychology: Sociological Perspectives*, New York: Basic Books

Henshel, Richard (1990). *Thinking About Social Problems*. New York: Harcourt Brace Jovanovich.

Horowitz, Ruth (1989). "Getting In." Carolyn Smith and William Kornblum (eds.). *In The Field: Readings on the Field Research Experience*. New York: Praeger.

Huff, Ronald (1986). "Home Detention as a Policy Alternative for Ohio's Juvenile Courts: A Final Report to the Governor's Office of Criminal Justice Services." Ohio: Unpublished Report.

Infantino, J.A. and S.Y. Musingo (1985). "Assaults and Injuries Among Staff With and Without Training in Aggression Control Techniques." *Hospital and Community Psychiatry*. Vol. 39 (12), pp. 1312-14.

Irwin, John (1980). *Prison in Turmoil*. Boston: Little, Brown & Company.

Jacobs, James (1977). *Stateville*. Chicago: Chicago University Press.

Johnson, John (1975). *Doing Field Research*. New York: Free Press.

Jorgensen, Danny L. (1989). *Participant Observation: A Methodology for Human Studies*. Newbury Park: Sage Publications.

Junker, Buford H. (1960). *Field Work: An Introduction to Social Sciences*. Chicago: University of Chicago Press.

Katz, Jack (1988). *Seductions of Crime: Moral and Sensual Attraction in Doing Evil*. New York: Basic Books.

Kauffman, Kelsey (1988). *Prison Officers and Their World*. Cambridge: Harvard University Press.

Keve, Paul and Casimir Zanick (1972). Final Report and Evaluation of the Home Detention Program, St Louis, Missouri, September 30 (1971) to July 1 (1972). McLean, VA: Research Analysis Corp.

Kobrin, Solomon and Malcolm Klein (1983). *Community Treatment of Juvenile Offenders: The DSO Experiments*. Beverly Hills: Sage Publications.

Krisberg, Barry (1988). *The Juvenile Court: Reclaiming the Vision*. San Francisco: National Council on Crime and Delinquency.

Landers, Robert K (1986). "Juvenile Justice Inside or Out." Hoyt Gimlin, Margaret Roberts, Richard Worsnop (eds.). In *Editorial Research Reports*. Vol. 2, pp 873-892.

Lemert, Edwin (1967). *Human Deviance, Social Problems and Social Control*. Englewood Cliffs, New Jersey: Prentice-Hall.

Lerman, Paul (1974). *Community Treatment and Social Control: A Critical Analysis of Juvenile Correctional Policy*. Chicago: University of Chicago Press.

Lerman, Paul (1982). *Destitutionalization and the Welfare State*. New Jersey: Rutgers University Press.

Lewis, Dan A., Stephanie Riger, Helen Rosenberg, Hendrik Wageraar, Authur Lurigio, Susan Reed (1991). *Worlds of the Mentally Ill: How Deinstitutionalization Works in the City*. Carbondale: Southern Illinois University Press.

Liska, Allen (1981). *Perspectives on Deviance*. New Jersey: Prentice-Hall.

Lipsky, Michael (1980). *Street-Level Bureaucracy: Dilemmas of the Individual in Public Service*. New York: Russell Sage.

Mann, Brenda J. and James Spradley (1975). *The Cocktail Waitress: Woman's Work in a Man's World*. New York: Alfred Knopf.

McDermott, Kathleen and Roy D. King (1988). "Mind Games: Where The Action is in Prison," *British Journal of Criminology*. Vol. 28, pp. 357-75.

McGarrell, Edmund (1988). *Juvenile Correctional Reform: Two Decades of Policy and Procedural Change*. Albany: State University of New York Press.

Meyer, R. (1980). "Attitudes of Parents of Institutionalized Mentally Retarded Individuals toward Deinstitutionalization." *American Journal of Mental Deficiency*. 85, 2, pp 184-187.

Morrissey, J.P. (1982). "Deinstitutionalizing the Mentally Ill: Process, Outcomes and New Directions." In W.R. Gove (ed.), *Deviance and Mental Illness*. Newbury Park, CA: Sage.

Owen, Barbara A. (1988). *The Reproduction of Social Control: A Study of Prison Workers at San Quentin*. New York: Preager.

Park, Robert (1969). *On Social Control and Collective Behavior*. Chicago: University of Chicago Press.

Parsons, Talcott (1967). *Sociological Theory and Modern Society*. NewYork: The Free Press.

_____. (1964). *The Social System*. The Free Press of Glencoe.

Polsky, Howard (1962). *Cottage Six: Social Systems of Delinquent Boys in Residential Treatment*. New York: Russell Sage Foundation.

Roesch, R and S.L. Golding (1985). "The Impact of Deinstitutionalization." In D.P. Farrington and J. Gunn (Eds.). *Aggression and Dangerous*. New York: John Wiley & Sons.

Scull, A.T. (1977). *Decarceration: Community Treatment and the Deviant: A Radical Review*. Englewood Cliffs, New Jersey: Prentice-Hall.

Smelser, Neil J. (1973). *Sociology: An Introduction*. 2nd Ed. New York: John Wiley and Sons.

Spencer, Jack (1987). "Probation Officer-Defendant Negotiations." In E. Rubington and M. Weinberg (eds.). *Deviance: The Interactionist Perspective* (5th ed.). New York: Macmillan Publishing Company.

Stone, A.A. (1982). "Psychiatric Abuse and Legal Reform: Two ways to make a bad situation worse." *International Journal of Law and Psychiatry*, 5, pp. 9-28.

Strauss, Anselm, Leonard Schatzman, Danuta Ehrlich, Rue Bucher, and Melvin Sabshin (1963). "The Hospital and Its Negotiated Order." Eliot Freidson (ed.). In *The Hospital in Modern Society*. New York: The Free Press of Glencoe.

Sykes, Gresham (1971). *Society of Captives.* New Jersey: Princeton University Press.

Warren, C. A. (1981). "New Forms of Social Control: The Myth of Deinstitutionalization." *American Behavioral Scientist,* 24 (6), pp. 724-740.

Wheeler, Stanton (1968). *Controlling Delinquents.* Ed., New York: Wiley.

Whitcomb, Edgar (1958). *Escape from Corregidor.* Chicago: H. Regnery Company.

Young, Thomas and Donnell Papperfort (1977). Secure Detention of Juveniles and Alternatives to its use. National Evaluation Program, Summary Report, Phase I. National Institute of Law Enforcement and Criminal Justice, LFAA. Washington, DC: Government Printing Office.

Index

About the Author

Paul-Jahi Christopher Price (Ph.D., UCLA) is Associate Professor of Sociology at Pasadena City College, Lecturer at California State University-Los Angeles, and Fullerton. E-mail: Pcprice@pasadena.edu.

A longtime advocate of students, Price has consistently advised students for fifteen years. He is advisor to the Black Student Alliance and Director of the African American Male Enrichment Program. Many of his students have completed undergraduate and graduate degrees becoming professionals of every type. Often, Price is asked to speak with high school students about attending college and career goals; moreover, Price speaks to public school teachers and churches about college, controlling youth and the civil rights movement.

This is Price's first book on *Social Control*, which evolved from his dissertation. It is a book rich with **control** theory and methods. He is currently working on *Sociology of Waiting*, a book that promises to stimulate and enlighten the sociological world. Price has written numerous articles for *The Pasadena/San Gabriel Valley Journal*, a local newspaper. Price enjoys writing for *The Journal* because his feedback is immediate, honest and thought provoking.

Price is the recipient of several awards; some of which include: Footsteps Award, American Sociological Association Minority Fellowship, Fisk University Graduate Fellowship and twice nominated for Outstanding Teacher Award at Pasadena City College. He has presented at several conferences including Pacific Sociological Association, Association of Black Sociologists, African American High School Conference and Flex Day Workshops at Pasadena City College. Finally, Price has made guest appearances on "Larry Mantle's *AirTalk*"

(KPCC) and Gerda Steele's "As We Speak"(Talk Television 56). KPCC and Talk Television 56 are local media emphasizing community development and involvement.

Price has served on several boards and committees. The African American Cultural Institute was especially meaningful to Price. This board developed and directed a Saturday school, which taught African American history and culture to elementary school students. Price was honored to serve on the Curriculum Integration Committee at Pasadena City College. Here, Price and others identified ways to diversify college curriculum and thus encouraged faculty to develop and use more inclusive course materials. No doubt, Price will continue working on boards and committees; his overriding concerns are providing meaningful participation and assistance to others.